THE CONSCIOUS LOVERS

by
Richard Steele

PLAYERS PRESS, Inc.
P.O. Box 1132
Studio City, CA 91614-0132

THE CONSCIOUS LOVERS

© Copyright, 1996, by William-Alan Landes
ISBN 0-88734-294-9
Library of Congress Catalogue Number: 96-12436

Library of Congress Cataloging-in-Publication Data

Steele, Richard, Sir, 1672-1729.
    The conscious lovers / by Richard Steele.
        p.   cm.
    ISBN 0-88734-294-9 (alk. paper)
    I. Title.
PR3704.C6   1996
822'.5--dc20

96-12436
CIP

INTRODUCTION

The eighteenth century saw the growth and eventual dominance of the middle class. With this new power came a weaker, less dominant theatre. The eminence of Elizabethan theatre had waned and, while it had seen some new strength in the Restoration's comedy of manners, this new view of ethics and everyday moral speculation brought drama almost to its knees.

Restoration comedy catered to the opposite extremes and centered about the aristocracy. It is not surprising to see drama sharply revolt and emphasize a bourgeois "moralizing of the stage." The aristocracy now preferred more fashionable amusements, such as the new Italian operas, and the lower classes did not go to the theatre or they preferred spectacular shows rather than drama.

The world presented through sentimental comedy is not the aristocratic world of the Restoration but a society of modes, of well-to-do humane and self-satisfied people. It sometimes scares me to see the parallels in the modern wealth within the English speaking middle class world of today.

In presenting this type of play upon the boards, comedy changed its fundamental nature. Instead of showing knavery and comic folly, it emphasized error, and dramatic writing deteriorated to a stylized formula. It was not enough to just say that comedy was acquiring a social purpose and shifting away from traditionalism; it was obviously taking over the theory of moral and human behavior.

Even in sermons and philosophical writings of the 1680's there was a softening of ethical theory. God, it stressed, was a God of love as well as of vengeance; our emotions and actions were pointed toward an approach at Divinity. Men were urged to experience the greatest of all joys, charity and good works. The older view of man still prevailed in some quarters; but in sentimental comedy, epitomized by the French Revolution, human nature was always seen as innately generous and quickly touched by altruistic emotions.

Steele is regarded as the true founder of sentimental comedy. In 1701, at the age of twenty-nine, he published a reforming tract –*The Christian Hero*– which elevated benevolence and a forgiving spirit to the bases of conduct. Shortly thereafter he emerged upon the theatrical world with his first comedy, *The Funeral*, which was followed by *The Lying Lover* (1703) and *The Tender Husband* (1705). Of these early plays *The Lying Lover* clearly shows the signs of sentimentality and is probably his best work.

The Conscious Lovers is a much later work (1722) and not Steele's best. But it clearly serves to illustrate the characteristics of early sentimental comedy better than most. The Preface asserts that "anything that has its foundation in happiness and success must be the object of comedy." Ironically Steele, the essayist, was a popular dramatist with his Good Friday sermon style which evoked significant literary criticism and controversy, upon which more rules were heaped. The critic Dennis vainly maintained "that a comedy without ridicule is unthinkable and that obviously comedy must concern itself with follies and vices if it is to be amusing."

From the point of view of dramatic art, sentimental comedy suffered a similar pattern as domestic tragedy. If a bourgeoise middle class drama –both comic and tragic– had its original roots in realism it was not encouraged to develop this realism to any specific conclusion. Instead of reality, this style only degenerated into another "ideal" form where watch words and labels became rules to replace characters and situations.

As with most empty theatrical experiences, thank you, it passed.

William-Alan Landes

4

DRAMATIS PERSONÆ

Men:

SIR JOHN BEVIL
MR. SEALAND
JOHN BEVIL JUNIOR, i*n love with* INDIANA
CHARLES MYRTLE, *in love with* LUCINDA
CIMBERTON, *a coxcomb*
HUMPHREY, *an old servant to* SIR JOHN
TOM, *servant to* BEVIL JUNIOR
DANIEL, *a country boy, servant to* INDIANA

Women:

MRS. SEALAND, *second wife to* SEALAND
ISABELLA, *sister to* SEALAND
INDIANA, SEALAND'S *daughter by his first wife*
LUCINDA, SEALAND'S *daughter by his second wife*
PHILLIS, *maid to* LUCINDA

SCENE: *London*

PROLOGUE

By MR. WELSTED

To win your hearts and to secure your praise,
The comic-writers strive by various ways:
By subtle stratagems they act their game,
And leave untry'd no avenue to fame.
One writes the spouse a beating from his wife,
And says each stroke was copy'd from the life.
Some fix all wit and humour in grimace,
And make a livelihood of Pinkey's face:
Here one gay show and costly habits tries,
Confiding to the judgment of your eyes:
Another smuts his scene (a cunning shaver),
Sure of the rakes' and of the wenches' favour.
Oft have these arts prevail'd; and, one may guess,
If practis'd o'er again, would find success.
But the bold sage, the poet of to-night,
By new and desp'rate rules resolv'd to write;
Fain would he give more just applauses rise,
And please by wit that scorns the aids of vice;
The praise he seeks from worthier motives springs,
Such praise as praise to those that give it brings.

Your aid, most humbly sought, then, Britons, lend,
And lib'ral mirth like lib'ral men defend:
No more let ribaldry, with licence writ,
Usurp the name of eloquence or wit;
No more let lawless farce uncensur'd go,
The lewd dull gleanings of a Smithfield show.
'Tis yours with breeding to refine the age,
To chasten wit, and moralize the stage.

Ye modest, wise and good, ye fair, ye brave,
To-night the champion of your virtues save;
Redeem from long contempt the comic name,
And judge politely for your country's fame.

THE CONSCIOUS LOVERS

ACT I

SCENE I

SCENE: SIR JOHN BEVIL's *house*
Enter SIR JOHN BEVIL *and* HUMPHREY

SIR J. BEV. Have you ordered that I should not be interrupted while I am dressing?

HUMPH. Yes, Sir: I believed you had something of moment to say to me.

SIR J. BEV. Let me see, Humphrey; I think it is now full forty years since I first took thee to be about myself.

HUMPH. I thank you, Sir; it has been an easy forty years, and I have passed 'em without much sickness, care, or labour.

SIR J. BEV. Thou hast a brave constitution; you are a year or two older than I am, Sirrah.

HUMPH. You have ever been of that mind, Sir.

SIR J. BEV. You knave, you know it; I took thee for thy gravity and sobriety, in my wild years.

HUMPH. Ah, Sir! our manners were formed from our different fortunes, not our different age. Wealth gave a loose to your youth, and poverty put a restraint upon mine.

SIR J. BEV. Well, Humphrey, you know I have been a kind master to you; I have used you, for the ingenious nature I observed in you from the beginning, more like an humble friend than a servant.

HUMPH. I humbly beg you'll be so tender of me as to explain your commands, Sir, without any farther preparation.

SIR J. BEV. I'll tell thee, then. In the first place, this wedding of my son's, in all probability (shut the door) will never be at all.

HUMPH. How, Sir! not be at all? For what reason is it carried on in appearance?

SIR J. BEV. Honest Humphrey, have patience, and I'll tell thee all in order. I have myself, in some part of my life, lived, indeed, with freedom, but, I hope, without reproach. Now, I

7

thought liberty would be as little injurious to my son; therefore, as soon as he grew towards man, I indulged him in living after his own manner: I knew not how, otherwise, to judge of his inclination; for what can be concluded from a behaviour under restraint and fear? But what charms me above all expression is that my son has never, in the least action, the most distant hint or word, valued himself upon that great estate of his mother's, which, according to our marriage settlement, he has had ever since he came to age.

HUMPH. No, Sir; on the contrary, he seems afraid of appearing to enjoy it before you or any belonging to you. He is as dependent and resigned to your will as if he had not a farthing but what must come from your immediate bounty. You have ever acted like a good and generous father, and he like an obedient and grateful son.

SIR J. BEV. Nay, his carriage is so easy to all with whom he converses, that he is never assuming, never prefers himself to others, nor ever is guilty of that rough sincerity which a man is not called to and certainly disobliges most of his acquaintance; to be short, Humphrey, his reputation was so fair in the world, that old Sealand, the great India merchant, has offered his only daughter and sole heiress to that vast estate of his, as a wife for him. You may be sure I made no difficulties; the match was agreed on, and this very day named for the wedding.

HUMPH. What hinders the proceeding?

SIR J. BEV. Don't interrupt me. You know I was last Thursday at the masquerade; my son, you may remember, soon found us out. He knew his grandfather's habit, which I then wore; and though it was the mode in the last age, yet the maskers, you know, followed us as if we had been the most monstrous figures in that whole assembly.

HUMPH. I remember, indeed, a young man of quality, in the habit of a clown, that was particularly troublesome.

SIR J. BEV. Right; he was too much what he seemed to be. You remember how impertinently he followed and teased us, and would know who we were.

HUMPH. (aside) I know he has a mind to come into that particular.

SIR J. BEV. Ay, he followed us till the gentleman who led the lady in the Indian mantle presented that gay creature to the rustic, and bid him (like Cymon in the fable) grow polite by falling in love, and let that worthy old gentleman alone—meaning me. The clown was not reformed, but rudely persisted, and offered to force off my mask; with that the gentleman, throwing off his own, appeared to be my son, and, in his concern for me, tore off that of the nobleman. At this they seized each other; the company called the guards; and in the surprise the lady swooned away; upon which my son quitted his adversary, and had now no care but of the lady—when, raising her in his arms, "Art thou gone," cried he, "forever?——

8

forbid it, heaven!" She revives at his known voice, and with the most familiar, though modest, gesture, hangs in safety over his shoulder weeping, but wept as in the arms of one before whom she could give herself a loose, were she not under observation. While she hides her face in his neck, he carefully conveys her from the company.

HUMPH. I have observed this accident has dwelt upon you very strongly.

SIR J. BEV. Her uncommon air, her noble modesty, the dignity of her person, and the occasion itself, drew the whole assembly together; and I soon heard it buzzed about, she was the adopted daughter of a famous sea-officer who had served in France. Now this unexpected and public discovery of my son's so deep concern for her——

HUMPH. Was what, I suppose, alarmed Mr. Sealand, in behalf of his daughter, to break off the match?

SIR J. BEV. You are right. He came to me yesterday and said he thought himself disengaged from the bargain, being credibly informed my son was already married, or worse, to the lady at the masquerade. I palliated matters, and insisted on our agreement; but we parted with little less than a direct breach between us.

HUMPH. Well, Sir; and what notice have you taken of all this to my young master?

SIR J. BEV. That's what I wanted to debate with you. I have said nothing to him yet. But look you, Humphrey—— if there is so much in this amour of his that he denies upon my summons to marry, I have cause enough to be offended; and then by my insisting upon his marrying to-day I shall know how far he is engaged to this lady in masquerade, and from thence only shall be able to take my measures. In the meantime I would have you find out how far that rogue, his man, is let into his secret. He, I know, will play tricks as much to cross me, as to serve his master.

HUMPH. Why do you think so of him, Sir? I believe he is no worse than I was for you at your son's age.

SIR J. BEV. I see it in the rascal's looks. But I have dwelt on these things too long; I'll go to my son immediately, and while I'm gone, your part is to convince his rogue Tom that I am in earnest. I'll leave him to you. (*Exit* SIR JOHN BEVIL)

HUMPH. Well, though this father and son live as well together as possible, yet their fear of giving each other pain is attended with constant mutual uneasiness. I'm sure I have enough to do to be honest and yet keep well with them both. But they know I love 'em, and that makes the task less painful, however.—— Oh, here's the prince of poor coxcombs, the representative of all the better fed than taught.—— Ho! ho! Tom, whither so gay and so airy this morning?

Enter TOM, *singing*

TOM. Sir, we servants of single gentlemen are another kind

9

of people than you domestic ordinary drudges that do business; we are raised above you. The pleasures of board-wages, tavern dinners, and many a clear gain—vails, alas! you never heard or dreamt of.

HUMPH. Thou hast follies and vices enough for a man of ten thousand a year, though 'tis but as t'other day that I sent for you to town to put you into Mr. Sealand's family, that you might learn a little before I put you to my young master, who is too gentle for training such a rude thing as you were into proper obedience. You then pulled off your hat to everyone you met in the street, like a bashful great awkward cub as you were. But your great oaken cudgel, when you were a booby, became you much better than that dangling stick at your button, now you are a fop. That's fit for nothing, except it hangs there to be ready for your master's hand when you are impertinent.

TOM. Uncle Humphrey, you know my master scorns to strike his servants. You talk as if the world was now just as it was when my old master and you were in your youth—when you went to dinner because it was so much o'clock, when the great blow was given in the hall at the pantry door, and all the family came out of their holes in such strange dresses and formal faces as you see in the pictures in our long gallery in the country.

HUMPH. Why, you wild rogue!

TOM. You could not fall to your dinner till a formal fellow in a black gown said something over the meat, as if the cook had not made it ready enough.

HUMPH. Sirrah, who do you prate after? Despising men of sacred characters! I hope you never heard my good young master talk so like a profligate.

TOM. Sir, I say you put upon me, when I first came to town, about being orderly, and the doctrine of wearing shams to make linen last clean a fortnight, keeping my clothes fresh, and wearing a frock within doors.

HUMPH. Sirrah, I gave you those lessons because I supposed at that time your master and you might have dined at home every day and cost you nothing; then you might have made a good family servant. But the gang you have frequented since at chocolate houses and taverns, in a continual round of noise and extravagance——

TOM. I don't know what you heavy inmates call noise and extravagance; but we gentlemen, who are well fed and cut a figure, Sir, think it a fine life, and that we must be very pretty fellows who are kept only to be looked at.

HUMPH. Very well, Sir! I hope the fashion of being lewd and extravagant, despising of decency and order, is almost at an end, since it is arrived at persons of your quality.

TOM. Master Humphrey, ha! ha! you were an unhappy lad to be sent up to town in such queer days as you were. Why now, Sir, the lackeys are the men of pleasure of the age, the top gamesters; and many a laced coat about town have had their education in our parti-coloured regiment. We are false lovers; have a taste of music, poetry, billets-doux, dress, politics; ruin damsels; and when we are weary of this lewd town and have a mind to take up, whip into our masters' wigs and linen, and marry fortunes.

HUMPH.   Hey-day!

TOM.   Nay, Sir, our order is carried up to the highest dignities and distinctions; step but into the Painted Chamber, and by our titles you'd take us all for men of quality. Then, again, come down to the Court of Requests, and you see us all laying our broken heads together for the good of the nation; and though we never carry a question *nemine contradicente,* yet this I can say with a safe conscience (and I wish every gentleman of our cloth could lay his hand upon his heart and say the same), that I never took so much as a single mug of beer for my vote in all my life.

HUMPH.   Sirrah, there is no enduring your extravagance; I'll hear you prate no longer. I wanted to see you to enquire how things go with your master, as far as you understand them; I suppose he knows he is to be married to-day.

TOM.   Ay, Sir, he knows it, and is dressed as gay as the sun; but, between you and I, my dear, he has a very heavy heart under all that gaiety. As soon as he was dressed I retired, but overheard him sigh in the most heavy manner. He walked thoughtfully to and fro in the room, then went into his closet; when he came out he gave me this for his mistress, whose maid, you know——

HUMPH.   Is passionately fond of your fine person.

TOM.   The poor fool is so tender, and loves to hear me talk of the world, and the plays, operas and ridottos for the winter, the parks and Belsize for our summer diversions; and "Lard!" says she, "you are so wild——but you have a world of humour."

HUMPH.   Coxcomb! Well, but why don't you run with your master's letter to Mrs. Lucinda, as he ordered you?

TOM.   Because Mrs. Lucinda is not so easily come at as you think for.

HUMPH.   Not easily come at? Why, Sirrah, are not her father and my old master agreed that she and Mr. Bevil are to be one flesh before to-morrow morning?

TOM.   It's no matter for that; her mother, it seems, Mrs. Sealand, has not agreed to it: and you must know, Mr. Humphrey, that in that family the grey mare is the better horse.

HUMPH.   What dost thou mean?

TOM.   In one word, Mrs. Sealand pretends to have a will of her own, and has provided a relation of hers, a stiff, starched philosopher and a wise fool, for her daughter; for which reason, for these ten days past, she has suffered no message nor letter from my master to come near her.

HUMPH. And where had you this intelligence?

TOM. From a foolish, fond soul that can keep nothing from me—one that will deliver this letter too, if she is rightly managed.

HUMPH. What! her pretty handmaid, Mrs. Phillis?

TOM. Even she, Sir; this is the very hour, you know, she usually comes hither, under a pretence of a visit to your housekeeper, forsooth, but in reality to have a glance at——

HUMPH. Your sweet face, I warrant you.

TOM. Nothing else in nature; you must know, I love to fret and play with the little wanton——

HUMPH. "Play with the little wanton!" What will this world come to!

TOM. I met her this morning in a new manteau and petticoat not a bit the worse for her lady's wearing, and she has always new thoughts and new airs with new clothes. Then, she never fails to steal some glance or gesture from every visitant at their house, and is, indeed, the whole town of coquettes at second hand.—— But here she comes; in one motion she speaks and describes herself better than all the words in the world can.

HUMPH. Then I hope, dear Sir, when your own affair is over, you will be so good as to mind your master's with her.

TOM. Dear Humphrey, you know my master is my friend, and those are people I never forget.

HUMPH. Sauciness itself! but I'll leave you to do your best for him.   (*Exit*)

Enter PHILLIS

PHIL. Oh, Mr. Thomas, is Mrs. Sugarkey at home? Lard! one is almost ashamed to pass along the streets. The town is quite empty, and nobody of fashion left in it; and the ordinary people do so stare to see anything dressed like a woman of condition, as it were, on the same floor with them, pass by. Alas! alas! it is a sad thing to walk. O Fortune! Fortune!

TOM. What! a sad thing to walk? Why, Madam Phillis, do you wish yourself lame?

PHIL. No, Mr. Tom, but I wish I were generally carried in a coach or chair, and of a fortune neither to stand nor go, but to totter, or slide, to be short-sighted, or stare, to fleer in the face, to look distant, to observe, to overlook, yet all become me; and if I was rich, I could twire and loll as well as the best of them. O Tom! Tom! is it not a pity that you should be so great a coxcomb, and I so great a coquette, and yet be such poor devils as we are?

TOM. Mrs. Phillis, I am your humble servant for that——

PHIL. Yes, Mr. Thomas, I know how much you are my humble servant, and know what you said to Mrs. Judy, upon seeing her in one of her lady's cast manteaus—that any one would have thought her the lady, and that she had ordered the other to wear it till it sat easy, for now only it was becoming—to my lady it was only a covering, to Mrs. Judy it was a habit. This you said, after somebody or other. O Tom! Tom! thou art as false and as base as the best gentleman of them all; but, you wretch, talk to me no more on the old odious subject. Don't, I say.

TOM (*in a submissive tone, retiring*)   I know not how to resist your commands, Madam.

PHIL.   Commands about parting are grown mighty easy to you of late.

TOM. (*aside*)   Oh, I have her; I have nettled and put her into the right temper to be wrought upon and set a-prating. —— Why, truly, to be plain with you, Mrs. Phillis, I can take little comfort of late in frequenting your house.

PHIL.   Pray, Mr. Thomas, what is it all of a sudden offends your nicety at our house?

TOM.   I don't care to speak particulars, but I dislike the whole.

PHIL.   I thank you, Sir, I am a part of that whole.

TOM.   Mistake me not, good Phillis.

PHIL.   Good Phillis! Saucy enough. But however——

TOM.   I say, it is that thou art a part which gives me pain for the disposition of the whole. You must know, Madam, to be serious, I am a man, at the bottom, of prodigious nice honour. You are too much exposed to company at your house. To be plain, I don't like so many, that would be your mistress's lovers, whispering to you.

PHIL.   Don't think to put that upon me. You say this because I wrung you to the heart when I touched your guilty conscience about Judy.

TOM.   Ah, Phillis! Phillis! if you but knew my heart!

PHIL.   I know too much on't.

TOM.   Nay, then, poor Crispo's fate and mine are one. Therefore give me leave to say, or sing at least, as he does upon the same occasion—   (*Sings*)

Se vedette, etc.

PHIL.   What, do you think I'm to be fobbed off with a song? I don't question but you have sung the same to Mrs. Judy too.

TOM.   Don't disparage your charms, good Phillis, with jealousy of so worthless an object; besides, she is a poor hussy, and if you doubt the sincerity of my love, you will allow me true to my interest. You are a fortune, Phillis——

PHIL.   What would the fop be at now? In good time, indeed, you shall be setting up for a fortune!

TOM.   Dear Mrs. Phillis, you have such a spirit that we shall never be dull in marriage when we come together. But I tell you, you are a fortune, and you have an estate in my hands.   (*He pulls out a purse; she eyes it*)

PHIL.   What pretence have I to what is in your hands, Mr. Tom?

13

TOM. As thus: there are hours, you know, when a lady is neither pleased or displeased, neither sick or well; when she lolls or loiters; when she's without desires, from having more of everything than she knows what to do with.

PHIL. Well, what then?

TOM. When she has not life enough to keep her bright eyes quite open, to look at her own dear image in the glass.

PHIL. Explain thyself, and don't be so fond of thy own prating.

TOM. There are also prosperous and good-natured moments, as when a knot or a patch is happily fixed, when the complexion particularly flourishes.

PHIL. Well, what then? I have not patience!

TOM. Why, then—or on the like occasions—we servants who have skill to know how to time business see when such a pretty folded thing as this (*shows a letter*) may be presented, laid, or dropped, as best suits the present humour. And, Madam, because it is a long, wearisome journey to run through all the several stages of a lady's temper, my master, who is the most reasonable man in the world, presents you this to bear your charges on the road. (*Gives her the purse*)

PHIL. Now you think me a corrupt hussy.

TOM. Oh, fie! I only think you'll take the letter.

PHIL. Nay, I know you do, but I know my own innocence; I take it for my mistress's sake.

TOM. I know it, my pretty one, I know it.

PHIL. Yes, I say, I do it because I would not have my mistress deluded by one who gives no proof of his passion; but I'll talk more of this as you see me on my way home. No, Tom, I assure thee I take this trash of thy master's, not for the value of the thing, but as it convinces me he has a true respect for my mistress. I remember a verse to the purpose:

They may be false who languish and complain,
But they who part with money never feign. (*Exeunt*)

SCENE II

SCENE: BEVIL JUNIOR'S *lodgings*

BEVIL JUNIOR, *reading*

BEV. JUN. These moral writers practise virtue after death. This charming Vision of Mirza! Such an author consulted in a morning sets the spirit for the vicissitudes of the day better than the glass does a man's person. But what a day have I to go through! to put on an easy look with an aching heart. If this lady my father urges me to marry should not refuse me, my dilemma is insupportable. But why should I fear it? is not she in equal distress with me? has not the letter I have sent her this morning confessed my inclination to another? Nay, have I not moral assurances of her engagements, too, to my friend

14

Myrtle? It's impossible but she must give in to it: for sure, to be denied is a favour any man may pretend to. It must be so. Well, then, with the assurance of being rejected, I think I may confidently say to my father I am ready to marry her. Then let me resolve upon—what I am not very good at, though it is—an honest dissimulation.

Enter TOM

TOM. Sir John Bevil, Sir, is in the next room.

BEV. JUN. Dunce! Why did not you bring him in?

TOM. I told him, Sir, you were in your closet.

BEV. JUN. I thought you had known, Sir, it was my duty to see my father anywhere.

(*going himself to the door*)

TOM. (*aside*) The devil's in my master! he has always more wit than I have.

BEV. JUN. (*introducing* SIR JOHN) Sir, you are the most gallant, the most complaisant of all parents. Sure, 'tis not a compliment to say these lodgings are yours. Why would you not walk in, Sir?

SIR J. BEV. I was loath to interrupt you unseasonably on your wedding-day.

BEV. JUN. One to whom I am beholden for my birthday might have used less ceremony.

SIR J. BEV. Well, Son, I have intelligence you have writ to your mistress this morning. It would please my curiosity to know the contents of a wedding-day letter, for courtship must then be over.

BEV. JUN. I assure you, Sir, there was no insolence in it upon the prospect of such a vast fortune's being added to our family, but much acknowledgment of the lady's greater desert.

SIR J. BEV. But, dear Jack, are you in earnest in all this? And will you really marry her?

BEV. JUN. Did I ever disobey any command of yours, Sir? nay, any inclination that I saw you bent upon?

SIR J. BEV. Why, I can't say you have, Son; but methinks in this whole business you have not been so warm as I could have wished you. You have visited her, it's true, but you have not been particular. Everyone knows you can say and do as handsome things as any man, but you have done nothing but lived in the general—been complaisant only.

BEV. JUN. As I am ever prepared to marry if you bid me, so I am ready to let it alone if you will have me.

HUMPHREY *enters, unobserved*

SIR J. BEV. Look you there now! Why, what am I to think of this so absolute and so indifferent a resignation?

BEV. JUN. Think? that I am still your son, Sir. Sir, you have been married, and I have not. And you have, Sir, found the inconvenience there is when a man weds with too much love in his head. I have been told, Sir, that at the time you mar-

15

ried, you made a mighty bustle on the occasion. There was challenging and fighting, scaling walls, locking up the lady, and the gallant under an arrest for fear of killing all his rivals. Now, Sir, I suppose you, having found the ill consequences of these strong passions and prejudices in preference of one woman to another, in case of a man's becoming a widower——

SIR J. BEV. How is this!

BEV. JUN. I say, Sir, experience has made you wiser in your care of me; for, Sir, since you lost my dear mother your time has been so heavy, so lonely, and so tasteless, that you are so good as to guard me against the like unhappiness, by marrying me prudentially by way of bargain and sale. For as you well judge, a woman that is espoused for a fortune is yet a better bargain if she dies; for then a man still enjoys what he did marry, the money, and is disencumbered of what he did not marry, the woman.

SIR J. BEV. But pray, Sir, do you think Lucinda, then, a woman of such little merit?

BEV. JUN. Pardon me, Sir, I don't carry it so far neither. I am rather afraid I shall like her too well; she has, for one of her fortune, a great many needless and superfluous good qualities.

SIR J. BEV. I am afraid, Son, there's something I don't see yet, something that's smothered under all this raillery.

BEV. JUN. Not in the least, Sir. If the lady is dressed and ready, you see I am. I suppose the lawyers are ready too.

HUMPH. (*aside*) This may grow warm if I don't interpose. —— Sir, Mr. Sealand is at the coffee-house, and has sent to speak with you.

SIR J. BEV. Oh, that's well! Then I warrant the lawyers are ready. Son, you'll be in the way, you say——

BEV. JUN. If you please, Sir, I'll take a chair, and go to Mr. Sealand's, where the young lady and I will wait your leisure.

SIR J. BEV. By no means. The old fellow will be so vain if he sees——

BEV. JUN. Ay; but the young lady, Sir, will think me so indifferent——

HUMPH. (*aside to* BEVIL JUNIOR) Ay, there you are right; press your readiness to go to the bride—he won't let you.

BEV. JUN. (*aside to* HUMPHREY) Are you sure of that?

HUMPH. (*aside*) How he likes being prevented!

SIR J. BEV. (*looking on his watch*) No, no. You are an hour or two too early.

BEV. JUN. You'll allow me, Sir, to think it too late to visit a beautiful, virtuous young woman, in the pride and bloom of life, ready to give herself to my arms; and to place her happiness or misery, for the future, in being agreeable or displeasing to me, is a—— Call a chair!

SIR J. BEV. No, no, no, dear Jack; this Sealand is a moody old fellow. There's no dealing with some people but by managing with indifference. We must leave to him the conduct of this day. It is the last of his commanding his daughter.

BEV. JUN.   Sir, he can't take it ill that I am impatient to be hers.

SIR J. BEV.   Pray, let me govern in this matter; you can't tell how humoursome old fellows are. There's no offering reason to some of 'em, especially when they are rich.—— (*aside*) If my son should see him before I've brought old Sealand into better temper, the match would be impracticable.

HUMPH.   Pray, Sir, let me beg you to let Mr. Bevil go.—— (*aside to* SIR JOHN) See whether he will or not—— (*then to* BEVIL JUNIOR) Pray, Sir, command yourself; since you see my master is positive, it is better you should not go.

BEV. JUN.   My father commands me as to the object of my affections, but I hope he will not as to the warmth and height of them.

SIR J. BEV. (*aside*)   So! I must even leave things as I found them, and in the meantime, at least, keep old Sealand out of his sight.——Well, Son, I'll go myself and take orders in your affair. You'll be in the way, I suppose, if I send to you. I'll leave your old friend with you.—— Humphrey, don't let him stir, d'ye hear?—— Your servant, your servant!

(*Exit* SIR JOHN BEVIL)

HUMPH.   I have a sad time on't, Sir, between you and my master. I see you are unwilling, and I know his violent inclinations for the match.—— I must betray neither and yet deceive you both, for your common good.—— Heaven grant a good end of this matter! But there is a lady, Sir, that gives your father much trouble and sorrow. You'll pardon me.

BEV. JUN.   Humphrey, I know thou art a friend to both, and in that confidence I dare tell thee——that lady is a woman of honour and virtue. You may assure yourself I never will marry without my father's consent. But give me leave to say, too, this declaration does not come up to a promise that I will take whosoever he pleases.

HUMPH.   Come, Sir, I wholly understand you. You would engage my services to free you from this woman whom my master intends you, to make way in time for the woman you have really a mind to.

BEV. JUN.   Honest Humphrey, you have always been an useful friend to my father and myself; I beg you, continue your good offices, and don't let us come to the necessity of a dispute; for, if we should dispute, I must either part with more than life, or lose the best of fathers.

HUMPH.   My dear master, were I but worthy to know this secret that so near concerns you, my life, my all should be engaged to serve you. This, Sir, I dare promise, that I am sure I will and can be secret. Your trust, at worst, but leaves you where you were; and if I cannot serve you, I will at once be plain and tell you so.

BEV. JUN.   That's all I ask. Thou hast made it now my interest to trust thee. Be patient, then, and hear the story of my heart.

HUMPH. I am all attention, Sir.

BEV. JUN. You may remember, Humphrey, that in my last travels my father grew uneasy at my making so long a stay at Toulon.

HUMPH. I remember it; he was apprehensive some woman had laid hold of you.

BEV. JUN. His fears were just, for there I first saw this lady. She is of English birth: her father's name was Danvers, a younger brother of an ancient family, and originally an eminent merchant of Bristol, who, upon repeated misfortunes, was reduced to go privately to the Indies. In this retreat Providence again grew favourable to his industry, and in six years' time restored him to his former fortunes. On this he sent directions over that his wife and little family should follow him to the Indies. His wife, impatient to obey such welcome orders, would not wait the leisure of a convoy, but took the first occasion of a single ship, and, with her husband's sister only, and this daughter, then scarce seven years old, undertook the fatal voyage—for here, poor creature, she lost her liberty and life; she and her family, with all they had, were unfortunately taken by a privateer from Toulon. Being thus made a prisoner, though as such not ill-treated, yet the fright, the shock, and cruel disappointment seized with such violence upon her unhealthy frame, she sickened, pined, and died at sea.

HUMPH. Poor soul! Oh, the helpless infant!

BEV. JUN. Her sister yet survived, and had the care of her. The captain, too, proved to have humanity, and became a father to her; for having himself married an English woman, and being childless, he brought home into Toulon this her little country-woman, presenting her, with all her dead mother's movables of value, to his wife, to be educated as his own adopted daughter.

HUMPH. Fortune here seemed again to smile on her.

BEV. JUN. Only to make her frowns more terrible; for in his height of fortune this captain, too, her benefactor, unfortunately was killed at sea, and, dying intestate, his estate fell wholly to an advocate, his brother, who, coming soon to take possession, there found, among his other riches, this blooming virgin at his mercy.

HUMPH. He durst not, sure, abuse his power!

BEV. JUN. No wonder if his pampered blood was fired at the sight of her—in short, he loved. But when all arts and gentle means had failed to move, he offered, too, his menaces in vain, denouncing vengeance on her cruelty, demanding her to account for all her maintenance from her childhood, seized on her little fortune as his own inheritance, and was dragging her by violence to prison, when Providence at the instant interposed, and sent me, by miracle, to relieve her.

HUMPH. 'Twas Providence, indeed. But pray, Sir, after all

this trouble how came this lady at last to England?

BEV. JUN. The disappointed advocate, finding she had so unexpected a support, on cooler thoughts descended to a composition, which I, without her knowledge, secretly discharged.

HUMPH. That generous concealment made the obligation double.

BEV. JUN. Having thus obtained her liberty, I prevailed, not without some difficulty, to see her safe to England, where no sooner arrived but my father, jealous of my being imprudently engaged, immediately proposed this other fatal match that hangs upon my quiet.

HUMPH. I find, Sir, you are irrecoverably fixed upon this lady.

BEV. JUN. As my vital life dwells in my heart; and yet you see what I do to please my father: walk in this pageantry of dress, this splendid covering of sorrow. But, Humphrey, you have your lesson.

HUMPH. Now, Sir, I have but one material question—

BEV. JUN. Ask it freely.

HUMPH. Is it, then, your own passion for this secret lady, or hers for you, that gives you this aversion to the match your father has proposed you?

BEV. JUN. I shall appear, Humphrey, more romantic in my answer than in all the rest of my story; for though I dote on her to death, and have no little reason to believe she has the same thoughts for me, yet in all my acquaintance and utmost privacies with her I never once directly told her that I loved.

HUMPH. How was it possible to avoid it?

BEV. JUN. My tender obligations to my father have laid so inviolable a restraint upon my conduct that till I have his consent to speak I am determined, on that subject, to be dumb forever.

HUMPH. Well, Sir, to your praise be it spoken, you are certainly the most unfashionable lover in Great Britain.

Enter TOM

TOM. Sir, Mr. Myrtle's at the next door, and, if you are at leisure, will be glad to wait on you.

BEV. JUN. Whenever he pleases.— Hold, Tom! did you receive no answer to my letter?

TOM. Sir, I was desired to call again, for I was told her mother would not let her be out of her sight. But about an hour hence, Mrs. Lettice said, I should certainly have one.

BEV. JUN. Very well.

HUMPH. Sir, I will take another opportunity: in the meantime, I only think it proper to tell you that, from a secret I know, you may appear to your father as forward as you please to marry Lucinda, without the least hazard of its coming to a conclusion. Sir, your most obedient servant!

BEV. JUN. Honest Humphrey, continue but my friend in this exigence and you shall always find me yours.

(*Exit* HUMPHREY)

I long to hear how my letter has succeeded with Lucinda——
but I think it cannot fail, for at worst, were it possible she
could take it ill, her resentment of my indifference may as
probably occasion a delay as her taking it right. Poor Myrtle,
what terrors must he be in all this while? Since he knows she
is offered to me and refused to him, there is no conversing or
taking any measures with him for his own service. But I ought
to bear with my friend, and use him as one in adversity:

All his disquiets by my own I prove;
The greatest grief's perplexity in love.   (*Exeunt*)

ACT II

Scene continues

Enter BEVIL JUNIOR *and* TOM

TOM. Sir, Mr. Myrtle.

BEV. JUN. Very well—do you step again, and wait for an answer to my letter.   (*Exit* TOM)

Enter MYRTLE

Well, Charles, why so much care in thy countenance? Is there anything in this world deserves it? You, who used to be so gay, so open, so vacant!

MYRT. I think we have of late changed complexions. You, who used to be much the graver man, are now all air in your behaviour. But the cause of my concern may, for aught I know, be the same object that gives you all this satisfaction. In a word, I am told that you are this very day—and your dress confirms me in it—to be married to Lucinda.

BEV. JUN. You are not misinformed. Nay, put not on the terrors of a rival till you hear me out. I shall disoblige the best of fathers if I don't seem ready to marry Lucinda; and you know I have ever told you you might make use of my secret resolution never to marry her, for your own service, as you please. But I am now driven to the extremity of immediately refusing or complying unless you help me to escape the match.

MYRT. Escape? Sir, neither her merit or her fortune are below your acceptance. Escaping do you call it!

BEV. JUN. Dear Sir, do you wish I should desire the match?

MYRT. No, but such is my humourous and sickly state of mind since it has been able to relish nothing but Lucinda, that though I must owe my happiness to your aversion to this marriage, I can't bear to hear her spoken of with levity or unconcern.

BEV. JUN. Pardon me, Sir; I shall transgress that way no more. She has understanding, beauty, shape, complexion, wit——

MYRT. Nay, dear Bevil, don't speak of her as if you loved her, neither.

BEV. JUN. Why, then, to give you ease at once, though I

21

allow Lucinda to have good sense, wit, beauty, and virtue, I know another in whom these qualities appear to me more amiable than in her.

MYRT. There you spoke like a reasonable and good-natured friend. When you acknowledge her merit and own your prepossession for another, at once you gratify my fondness and cure my jealousy.

BEV. JUN. But all this while you take no notice, you have no apprehension, of another man that has twice the fortune of either of us.

MYRT. Cimberton! Hang him, a formal, philosophical, pedantic coxcomb! for the sot, with all these crude notions of divers things, under the direction of great vanity and very little judgment, shows his strongest bias is avarice; which is so predominant in him that he will examine the limbs of his mistress with the caution of a jockey, and pays no more compliment to her personal charms than if she were a mere breeding animal.

BEV. JUN. Are you sure that is not affected? I have known some women sooner set on fire by that sort of negligence than by——

MYRT. No, no! hang him, the rogue has no art; it is pure, simple insolence and stupidity.

BEV. JUN. Yet with all this, I don't take him for a fool.

MYRT. I own the man is not a natural; he has a very quick sense, though very slow understanding. He says, indeed, many things that want only the circumstances of time and place to be very just and agreeable.

BEV. JUN. Well, you may be sure of me if you can disappoint him; but my intelligence says the mother has actually sent for the conveyancer to draw articles for his marriage with Lucinda, though those for mine with her are, by her father's order, ready for signing. But it seems she has not thought fit to consult either him or his daughter in the matter.

MYRT. Pshaw! a poor, troublesome woman. Neither Lucinda nor her father will ever be brought to comply with it; besides, I am sure Cimberton can make no settlement upon her without the concurrence of his great-uncle, Sir Geoffry, in the west.

BEV. JUN. Well, Sir, and I can tell you that's the very point that is now laid before her counsel, to know whether a firm settlement can be made without this uncle's actual joining in it. Now pray consider, Sir, when my affair with Lucinda comes, as it soon must, to an open rupture, how are you sure that Cimberton's fortune may not then tempt her father, too, to hear his proposals?

MYRT. There you are right, indeed; that must be provided against. Do you know who are her counsel?

BEV. JUN. Yes, for your service I have found out that, too: they are Sergeant Bramble and old Target——by the way, they are neither of 'em known in the family. Now, I was thinking why you might not put a couple of false counsel upon her to delay and confound matters a little; besides, it may probably let you into the bottom of her whole design against you.

MYRT. As how, pray?

BEV. JUN. Why, can't you slip on a black wig and a gown, and be old Bramble yourself?

MYRT. Ha! I don't dislike it. But what shall I do for a brother in the case?

BEV. JUN. What think you of my fellow Tom? The rogue's intelligent, and is a good mimic. All his part will be but to stutter heartily, for that's old Target's case. Nay, it would be an immoral thing to mock him, were it not that his impertinence is the occasion of its breaking out to that degree. The conduct of the scene will chiefly lie upon you.

MYRT. I like it of all things; if you'll send Tom to my chambers I will give him full instructions. This will certainly give me occasion to raise difficulties, to puzzle or confound her project for a while at least.

BEV. JUN. I'll warrant you success: so far we are right, then. And now, Charles, your apprehension of my marrying her is all you have to get over.

MYRT. Dear Bevil! though I know you are my friend, yet when I abstract myself from my own interest in the thing, I know no objection she can make to you or you to her, and therefore hope——

BEV. JUN. Dear Myrtle, I am as much obliged to you for the cause of your suspicion as I am offended at the effect: but be assured, I am taking measures for your certain security, and that all things with regard to me will end in your entire satisfaction.

MYRT. Well, I'll promise you to be as easy and as confident as I can, though I cannot but remember that I have more than life at stake on your fidelity.   (*going*)

BEV. JUN. Then depend upon it, you have no chance against you.

MYRT. Nay, no ceremony; you know I must be going.

(*Exit* MYRTLE)

BEV. JUN. Well! this is another instance of the perplexities which arise, too, in faithful friendship. We must often in this life go on in our good offices even under the displeasure of those to whom we do them, in compassion to their weaknesses and mistakes. But all this while poor Indiana is tortured with the doubt of me! She has no support or comfort but in my fidelity, yet sees me daily pressed to marriage with another! How painful, in such a crisis, must be every hour she thinks on me! I'll let her see at least my conduct to her is not changed. I'll take this opportunity to visit her; for though the religious vow I have made to my father restrains me from ever marrying without his approbation, yet that confines me not from seeing a virtuous woman that is the pure delight of my eyes and the guiltless joy of my heart. But the best condi-

23

tion of human life is but a gentler misery.

   To hope for perfect happiness is vain,
   And love has ever its allays of pain.   (*Exit*)

Enter ISABELLA *and* INDIANA *in her own lodgings*

ISAB.   Yes, I say 'tis artifice, dear child: I say to thee again and again, 'tis all skill and management.

IND.   Will you persuade me there can be an ill design in supporting me in the condition of a woman of quality? attended, dressed, and lodged like one—in my appearance abroad and my furniture at home, every way in the most sumptuous manner—and he that does it has an artifice, a design in it?

ISAB.   Yes, yes.

IND.   And all this without so much as explaining to me that all about me comes from him!

ISAB.   Ay, ay, the more for that. That keeps the title to all you have the more in him.

IND.   The more in him! He scorns the thought——

ISAB.   Then he—— He—— He——

IND.   Well, be not so eager. If he is an ill man, let us look into his stratagems. Here is another of them. (*showing a letter*)   Here's two hundred and fifty pound in bank notes, with these words: "To pay for the set of dressing-plate which will be brought home to-morrow." Why, dear Aunt, now here's another piece of skill for you, which I own I cannot comprehend, and it is with a bleeding heart I hear you say anything to the disadvantage of Mr. Bevil. When he is present I look upon him as one to whom I owe my life and the support of it —then, again, as the man who loves me with sincerity and honour. When his eyes are cast another way and I dare survey him, my heart is painfully divided between shame and love. Oh! could I tell you——

ISAB.   Ah! you need not: I imagine all this for you.

IND.   This is my state of mind in his presence, and when he is absent, you are ever dinning my ears with notions of the arts of men; that his hidden bounty, his respectful conduct, his careful provision for me, after his preserving me from utmost misery, are certain signs he means nothing but to make I know not what of me.

ISAB.   Oh! You have a sweet opinion of him, truly.

IND.   I have, when I am with him, ten thousand things, besides my sex's natural decency and shame, to suppress my heart, that yearns to thank, to praise, to say it loves him. I say, thus it is with me while I see him; and in his absence I am entertained with nothing but your endeavours to tear this amiable image from my heart and in its stead to place a base dissembler, an artful invader of my happiness, my innocence, my honour.

ISAB. Ah, poor soul! has not his plot taken? don't you die for him? has not the way he has taken been the most proper with you? Oh! ho! He has sense, and has judged the thing right.

IND. Go on, then, since nothing can answer you; say what you will of him. Heigh! ho!

ISAB. Heigh! ho! indeed. It is better to say so, as you are now, than as many others are. There are, among the destroyers of women, the gentle, the generous, the mild, the affable, the humble, who all, soon after their success in their designs, turn to the contrary of those characters. I will own to you, Mr. Bevil carries his hypocrisy the best of any man living, but still he is a man, and therefore a hypocrite. They have usurped an exemption from shame for any baseness, any cruelty towards us. They embrace without love; they make vows without conscience of obligation; they are partners, nay, seducers to the crime wherein they pretend to be less guilty.

IND. (*aside*) That's truly observed.—— But what's all this to Bevil?

ISAB. This it is to Bevil and all mankind. Trust not those who will think the worse of you for your confidence in them—serpents who lie in wait for doves. Won't you be on your guard against those who would betray you? Won't you doubt those who would contemn you for believing 'em? Take it from me: fair and natural dealing is to invite injuries; 'tis bleating to escape wolves who would devour you! Such is the world—— (*aside*) and such (since the behaviour of one man to myself) have I believed all the rest of the sex.

IND. I will not doubt the truth of Bevil; I will not doubt it. He has not spoke it by an organ that is given to lying; his eyes are all that have ever told me that he was mine. I know his virtue, I know his filial piety, and ought to trust his management with a father to whom he has uncommon obligations. What have I to be concerned for? my lesson is very short. If he takes me forever, my purpose of life is only to please him. If he leaves me (which heaven avert), I know he'll do it nobly, and I shall have nothing to do but to learn to die, after worse than death has happened to me.

ISAB. Ay do, persist in your credulity! Flatter yourself that a man of his figure and fortune will make himself the jest of the town, and marry a handsome beggar for love.

IND. The town! I must tell you, Madam, the fools that laugh at Mr. Bevil will but make themselves more ridiculous; his actions are the result of thinking, and he has sense enough to make even virtue fashionable.

ISAB. O' my conscience, he has turned her head. Come, come; if he were the honest fool you take him for, why has he kept you here these three weeks without sending you to Bristol in search of your father, your family, and your relations?

IND. I am convinced he still designs it, and that nothing keeps him here but the necessity of not coming to a breach with his father in regard to the match he has proposed him. Beside, has he not writ to Bristol? and has not he advice that my father has not been heard of there almost these twenty years?

ISAB. All sham, mere evasion; he is afraid if he should carry you hither, your honest relations may take you out of his hands and so blow up all his wicked hopes at once.

IND. Wicked hopes! did I ever give him any such?

ISAB. Has he ever given you any honest ones? Can you say, in your conscience, he has ever once offered to marry you?

IND. No! but by his behaviour I am convinced he will offer it the moment 'tis in his power, or consistent with his honour, to make such a promise good to me.

ISAB. His honour!

IND. I will rely upon it; therefore desire you will not make my life uneasy by these ungrateful jealousies of one to whom I am, and wish to be, obliged, for from his integrity alone I have resolved to hope for happiness.

ISAB. Nay, I have done my duty; if you won't see, at your peril be it.

IND. Let it be.—— This is his hour of visiting me.

ISAB. (*apart*) Oh! to be sure, keep up your form; don't see him in a bed-chamber. This is pure prudence, when she is liable, wherever he meets her, to be conveyed where'er he pleases.

IND. All the rest of my life is but waiting till he comes: I live only when I'm with him. (*Exit*)

ISAB. Well, go thy ways, thou wilful innocent! I once had almost as much love for a man who poorly left me to marry an estate—and I am now, against my will, what they call an old maid: but I will not let the peevishness of that condition grow upon me; only keep up the suspicion of it, to prevent this creature's being any other than a virgin, except upon proper terms. (*Exit*)

Re-enter INDIANA, *speaking to a Servant*

IND. Desire Mr. Bevil to walk in.—— Design! impossible! A base, designing mind could never think of what he hourly puts in practice. And yet, since the late rumour of his marriage, he seems more reserved than formerly; he sends in, too, before he sees me, to know if I am at leisure. Such new respect may cover coldness in the heart—it certainly makes me thoughtful. I'll know the worst at once; I'll lay such fair occasions in his way that it shall be impossible to avoid an explanation, for these doubts are insupportable.—— But see! he comes and clears them all.

Enter BEVIL JUNIOR

BEV. JUN. Madam, your most obedient! I am afraid I

broke in upon your rest last night—'twas very late before we parted, but 'twas your own fault: I never saw you in such agreeable humour.

IND. I am extremely glad we were both pleased, for I thought I never saw you better company.

BEV. JUN. Me, Madam! you rally; I said very little.

IND. But I am afraid you heard me say a great deal; and, when a woman is in the talking vein, the most agreeable thing a man can do, you know, is to have patience to hear her.

BEV. JUN. Then it's pity, Madam, you should ever be silent, that we might be always agreeable to one another.

IND. If I had your talent or power to make my actions speak for me, I might indeed be silent, and yet pretend to something more than the agreeable.

BEV. JUN. If I might be vain of anything in my power, Madam, 'tis that my understanding from all your sex has marked you out as the most deserving object of my esteem.

IND. Should I think I deserve this, 'twere enough to make my vanity forfeit the very esteem you offer me.

BEV. JUN. How so, Madam?

IND. Because esteem is the result of reason, and to deserve it from good sense, the height of human glory. Nay, I had rather a man of honour should pay me that, than all the homage of a sincere and humble love.

BEV. JUN. You certainly distinguish right, Madam; love often kindles from external merit only——

IND. But esteem arises from a higher source, the merit of the soul.

BEV. JUN. True, and great souls only can deserve it.

(bowing respectfully)

IND. Now I think they are greater still that can so charitably part with it.

BEV. JUN. Now, Madam, you make me vain, since the utmost pride and pleasure of my life is that I esteem you—as I ought.

IND. *(aside)* As he ought! Still more perplexing! He neither saves nor kills my hope.

BEV. JUN. But, Madam, we grow grave, methinks. Let's find some other subject. Pray, how did you like the opera last night?

IND. First give me leave to thank you for my tickets.

BEV. JUN. Oh, your servant, Madam! But pray tell me; you, now, who are never partial to the fashion, I fancy, must be the properest judge of a mighty dispute among the ladies, that is, whether *Crispo* or *Griselda* is the more agreeable entertainment.

IND. With submission, now, I cannot be a proper judge of this question.

BEV. JUN. How so, Madam?

IND. Because I find I have a partiality for one of them.

BEV. JUN. Pray, which is that?

27

IND. I do not know—there's something in that rural cottage of Griselda, her forlorn condition, her poverty, her solitude, her resignation, her innocent slumbers, and that lulling *Dolce sogno* that's sung over her; it had an effect upon me that—— in short, I never was so well deceived at any of them.

BEV. JUN. Oh! Now, then, I can account for the dispute: *Griselda*, it seems, is the distress of an injured, innocent woman; *Crispo*, that only of a man in the same condition; therefore the men are mostly concerned for Crispo, and, by a natural indulgence, both sexes for Griselda.

IND. So that judgment, you think, ought to be for one, though fancy and complaisance have got ground for the other. Well! I believe you will never give me leave to dispute with you on any subject, for I own *Crispo* has its charms for me too, though in the main all the pleasure the best opera gives us is but mere sensation. Methinks it's pity the mind can't have a little more share in the entertainment. The music's certainly fine, but, in my thoughts, there's none of your composers come up to old Shakespeare and Otway.

BEV. JUN. How, Madam! Why, if a woman of your sense were to say this in the drawing-room——

Enter a Servant

SERV. Sir, here's Signor Carbonelli says he waits your commands in the next room.

BEV. JUN. A propos! You were saying yesterday, Madam, you had a mind to hear him; will you give him leave to entertain you now?

IND. By all means.—— Desire the gentleman to walk in.

(*Exit Servant*)

BEV. JUN. I fancy you will find something in this hand that is uncommon.

IND. You are always finding ways, Mr. Bevil, to make life seem less tedious to me.

Enter Music Master

When the gentleman pleases.

(*After a sonata is played,* BEVIL *waits on the Master to the door, etc.*)

BEV. JUN. You smile, Madam, to see me so complaisant to one whom I pay for his visit. Now I own I think it is not enough barely to pay those whose talents are superior to our own (I mean such talents as would become our condition, if we had them). Methinks we ought to do something more than barely gratify them for what they do at our command only because their fortune is below us.

IND. You say I smile: I assure you it was a smile of approbation; for indeed, I cannot but think it the distinguishing part of a gentleman to make his superiority of fortune as easy to his inferiors as he can.—— (*aside*) Now once more to try him. —— I was saying just now, I believed you would never let me

28

dispute with you, and I daresay it will always be so. However, I must have your opinion upon a subject which created a debate between my aunt and me just before you came hither. She would needs have it that no man every does any extraordinary kindness or service for a woman but for his own sake.

BEV. JUN. Well, Madam! Indeed, I can't but be of her mind.

IND. What, though he should maintain and support her, without demanding anything of her on her part?

BEV. JUN. Why, Madam, is making an expense in the service of a valuable woman (for such I must suppose her), though she should never do him any favour—nay, though she should never know who did her such service—such a mighty heroic business?

IND. Certainly! I should think he must be a man of an uncommon mould.

BEV. JUN. Dear Madam, why so? 'tis but, at best, a better taste in expense. To bestow upon one whom he may think one of the ornaments of the whole creation; to be conscious that from his superfluity an innocent, a virtuous spirit is supported above the temptations and sorrows of life! That he sees satisfaction, health, and gladness in her countenance, while he enjoys the happiness of seeing her (as that I will suppose too, or he must be too abstracted, too insensible)—— I say, if he is allowed to delight in that prospect, alas! what mighty matter is there in all this?

IND. No mighty matter in so disinterested a friendship!

BEV. JUN. Disinterested! I can't think him so. Your hero, Madam, is no more than what every gentleman ought to be and I believe very many are. He is only one who takes more delight in reflections than in sensations. He is more pleased with thinking than eating; that's the utmost you can say of him. Why, Madam, a greater expense than all this men lay out upon an unnecessary stable of horses.

IND. Can you be sincere in what you say?

BEV. JUN. You may depend upon it, if you know any such man, he does not love dogs inordinately.

IND. No, that he does not.

BEV. JUN. Nor cards, nor dice.

IND. No.

BEV. JUN. Nor bottle companions.

IND. No.

BEV. JUN. Nor loose women.

IND. No, I'm sure he does not.

BEV. JUN. Take my word, then, if your admired hero is not liable to any of these kind of demands, there's no such preeminence in this as you imagine. Nay, this way of expense you speak of is what exalts and raises him that has a taste for it; and, at the same time, his delight is incapable of satiety, disgust, or penitence.

IND. But still I insist, his having no private interest in the

29

action makes it prodigious, almost incredible.

BEV. JUN.　Dear Madam, I never knew you more mistaken. Why, who can be more a usurer than he who lays out his money in such valuable purchases? If pleasure be worth purchasing, how great a pleasure is it, to him who has a true taste of life, to ease an aching heart, to see the human countenance lighted up into smiles of joy, on the receipt of a bit of ore which is superfluous and otherwise useless in a man's own pocket? What could a man do better with his cash? This is the effect of a humane disposition where there is only a general tie of nature and common necessity. What then must it be when we serve an object of merit, of admiration!

IND.　Well! the more you argue against it, the more I shall admire the generosity.

BEV. JUN.　Nay, nay!——then, Madam, 'tis time to fly, after a declaration that my opinion strengthens my adversary's argument. I had best hasten to my appointment with Mr. Myrtle, and be gone while we are friends and—before things are brought to an extremity.　　　(*Exit carelessly*)

Enter ISABELLA

ISAB.　Well, Madam, what think you of him now, pray?

IND.　I protest, I begin to fear he is wholly disinterested in what he does for me. On my heart, he has no other view but the mere pleasure of doing it, and has neither good or bad designs upon me.

ISAB.　Oh! dear Niece! don't be in fear of both! I'll warrant you, you will know time enough that he is not indifferent.

IND.　You please me when you tell me so, for if he has any wishes towards me I know he will not pursue them but with honour.

ISAB.　I wish I were as confident of one as t'other. I saw the respectful downcast of his eye when you catched him gazing at you during the music. He, I warrant, was surprised, as if he had been taken stealing your watch. Oh, the undissembled, guilty look!

IND.　But did you observe any such thing, really? I thought he looked most charmingly graceful! How engaging is modesty in a man when one knows there is a great mind within. So tender a confusion! and yet, in other respects, so much himself, so collected, so dauntless, so determined!

ISAB.　Ah, Niece! there is a sort of bashfulness which is the best engine to carry on a shameless purpose: some men's modesty serves their wickedness, as hypocrisy gains the respect due to piety. But I will own to you, there is one hopeful symptom, if there could be such a thing as a distinterested lover. But it's all a perplexity, till—— till—— till——

IND.　Till what?

ISAB.　Till I know whether Mr. Myrtle and Mr. Bevil are really friends or foes. And that I will be convinced of before I sleep, for you shall not be deceived.

30

IND. I'm sure I never shall if your fears can guard me. In the meantime I'll wrap myself up in the integrity of my own heart, nor dare to doubt of his.

As conscious honour all his actions steers,
So conscious innocence dispels my fears.   (*Exeunt*)

ACT III

Enter TOM, *meeting* PHILLIS

TOM. Well, Phillis!—what, with a face as if you had never seen me before!—— (*aside*) What a work have I to do now? She has seen some new visitant at their house, whose airs she has catched, and is resolved to practise them upon me. Numberless are the changes she'll dance through before she'll answer this plain question, videlicet, "Have you delivered my master's letter to your lady?" Nay, I know her too well to ask an account of it in an ordinary way; I'll be in my airs as well as she.—— (*looking steadfastly at her*) Well, Madam, as unhappy as you are at present pleased to make me, I would not, in the general, be any other than what I am; I would not be a bit wiser, a bit richer, a bit taller, a bit shorter than I am at this instant.

PHIL. Did ever anybody doubt, Master Thomas, but that you were extremely satisfied with your sweet self?

TOM. I am, indeed. The thing I have least reason to be satisfied with is my fortune, and I am glad of my poverty. Perhaps if I were rich I should overlook the finest woman in the world, that wants nothing but riches to be thought so.

PHIL. (*aside*) How prettily was that said! But I'll have a great deal more before I'll say one word.

TOM. I should, perhaps, have been stupidly above her, had I not been her equal, and by not being her equal, never had opportunity of being her slave. I am my master's servant for hire; I am my mistress's from choice, would she but approve my passion.

PHIL. I think it's the first time I ever heard you speak of it with any sense of the anguish, if you really do suffer any.

TOM. Ah, Phillis! can you doubt, after what you have seen?

PHIL. I know not what I have seen, nor what I have heard; but since I'm at leisure, you may tell me when you fell in love with me, how you fell in love with me, and what you have suffered or are ready to suffer for me.

TOM. (*aside*) Oh, the unmerciful jade! when I'm in haste about my master's letter. But I must go through it.—— Ah! too well I remember when, and how, and on what occasion I was

32

first surprised. It was on the first of April, one thousand seven hundred and fifteen, I came into Mr. Sealand's service; I was then a hobbledehoy, and you a pretty little tight girl, a favourite handmaid of the housekeeper. At that time we neither of us knew what was in us. I remember I was ordered to get out the window, one pair of stairs, to rub the sashes clean; the person employed on the inner side was your charming self, whom I had never seen before.

PHIL.   I think I remember the silly accident. What made ye, you oaf, ready to fall down into the street?

TOM.   You know not, I warrant you. You could not guess what surprised me. You took no delight when you immediately grew wanton in your conquest, and put your lips close and breathed upon the glass, and when my lips approached, a dirty cloth you rubbed against my face, and hid your beauteous form; when I again drew near, you spit, and rubbed, and smiled at my undoing.

PHIL.   What silly thoughts you men have!

TOM.   We were Pyramus and Thisbe—but ten times harder was my fate. Pyramus could peep only through a wall; I saw her, saw my Thisbe in all her beauty, but as much kept from her as if a hundred walls between, for there was more, there was her will against me. Would she but yet relent! O Phillis! Phillis! shorten my torment and declare you pity me.

PHIL.   I believe it's very sufferable; the pain is not so exquisite but that you may bear it a little longer.

TOM.   Oh, my charming Phillis! if all depended on my fair one's will, I could with glory suffer. But, dearest creature, consider our miserable state.

PHIL.   How! Miserable!

TOM.   We are miserable to be in love and under the command of others than those we love—with that generous passion in the heart, to be sent to and fro on errands, called, checked, and rated for the meanest trifles. O Phillis! you don't know how many china cups and glasses my passion for you has made me break. You have broke my fortune as well as my heart.

PHIL.   Well, Mr. Thomas, I cannot but own to you that I believe your master writes and you speak the best of any men in the world. Never was woman so well pleased with a letter as my young lady was with his, and this is an answer to it.

(*Gives him a letter*)

TOM.   This was well done, my dearest. Consider, we must strike out some pretty livelihood for ourselves by closing their affairs. It will be nothing for them to give us a little being of our own, some small tenement, out of their large possessions: whatever they give us, 'twill be more than what they keep for themselves: one acre with Phillis would be worth a whole county without her.

PHIL.   Oh, could I but believe you!

TOM.   If not the utterance, believe the touch of my lips.

(Kisses her)

PHIL. There's no contradicting you; how closely you argue, Tom!

TOM. And will closer, in due time. But I must hasten with this letter, to hasten towards the possession of you. Then, Phillis, consider how I must be revenged, look to it, of all your skittishness, shy looks, and at best but coy compliances.

PHIL. O Tom! you grow wanton and sensual, as my lady calls it; I must not endure it. Oh! Foh! you are a man, an odious, filthy male creature; you should behave, if you had a right sense or were a man of sense, like Mr. Cimberton, with distance and indifference, or—let me see—some other becoming hard word, with seeming in-in-inadvertency, and not rush on one as if you were seizing a prey.—— But hush! the ladies are coming.—— Good Tom, don't kiss me above once, and be gone. Lard! we have been fooling and toying, and not considered the main business of our masters and mistresses.

TOM. Why, their business is to be fooling and toying as soon as the parchments are ready.

PHIL. Well remembered—— parchments! My lady, to my knowledge, is preparing writings between her coxcomb cousin, Cimberton, and my mistress, though my master has an eye to the parchments already prepared between your master, Mr. Bevil, and my mistress; and, I believe, my mistress herself has signed and sealed, in her heart, to Mr. Myrtle.—— Did I not bid you kiss me but once, and be gone? but I know you won't be satisfied.

TOM. *(kissing her hand)* No, you smooth creature, how should I!

PHIL. Well, since you are so humble, or so cool, as to ravish my hand only, I'll take my leave of you like a great lady, and you a man of quality. *(They salute formally)*

TOM. Pox of all this state!

(offers to kiss her more closely)

PHIL. No, prithee, Tom, mind your business! We must follow that interest which will take, but endeavour at that which will be most for us and we like most. Oh, here's my young mistress! (TOM *taps her neck behind, and kisses his fingers.)* Go, ye liquorish fool! *(Exit TOM)*

Enter LUCINDA

LUC. Who was that you was hurrying away?

PHIL. One that I had no mind to part with.

LUC. Why did you turn him away then?

PHIL. For your ladyship's service, to carry your ladyship's letter to his master. I could hardly get the rogue away.

LUC. Why, has he so little love for his master?

PHIL. No; but he has so much love for his mistress.

LUC. But I thought I heard him kiss you. Why do you suffer that?

PHIL. Why, Madam, we vulgar take it to be a sign of love.

34

We servants, we poor people, that have nothing but our persons to bestow or treat for, are forced to deal and bargain by way of sample, and therefore, as we have no parchments or wax necessary in our agreements, we squeeze with our hands and seal with our lips to ratify vows and promises.

LUC. But can't you trust one another without such earnest down?

PHIL. We don't think it safe, any more than you gentry, to come together without deeds executed.

LUC. Thou art a pert, merry hussy.

PHIL. I wish, Madam, your lover and you were as happy as Tom and your servant are.

LUC. You grow impertinent.

PHIL. I have done, Madam; and I won't ask you what you intend to do with Mr. Myrtle, what your father will do with Mr. Bevil, nor what you all, especially my lady, mean by admitting Mr. Cimberton as particularly here as if he were married to you already; nay, you are married actually as far as people of quality are.

LUC. How's that?

PHIL. You have different beds in the same house.

LUC. Pshaw! I have a very great value for Mr. Bevil, but have absolutely put an end to his pretensions in the letter I gave you for him. But my father, in his heart, still has a mind to him, were it not for this woman they talk of; and I am apt to imagine he is married to her, or never designs to marry at all.

PHIL. Then Mr. Myrtle——

LUC. He had my parents' leave to apply to me, and by that has won me and my affections: who is to have this body of mine without 'em, it seems, is nothing to me. My mother says it's indecent for me to let my thoughts stray about the person of my husband; nay, she says a maid, rigidly virtuous, though she may have been where her lover was a thousand times, should not have made observations enough to know him from another man when she sees him in a third place.

PHIL. That is more than the severity of a nun, for not to see when one may is hardly possible; not to see when one can't is very easy. At this rate, Madam, there are a great many whom you have not seen who——

LUC. Mamma says the first time you see your husband should be at that instant he is made so, when your father, with the help of the minister, gives you to him; then you are to see him, then you are to observe and take notice of him, because then you are to obey him.

PHIL. But does not my lady remember you are to love as well as obey?

LUC. To love is a passion, 'tis a desire, and we must have no desires. Oh! I cannot endure the reflection! With what insensibility on my part, with what more than patience, have I been exposed and offered to some awkward booby or other in every county of Great Britain!

PHIL.   Indeed, Madam, I wonder I never heard you speak of it before with this indignation.

LUC.   Every corner of the land has presented me with a wealthy coxcomb. As fast as one treaty has gone off, another has come on, till my name and person have been the tittle-tattle of the whole town. What is this world come to! No shame left! To be bartered for like the beasts of the fields, and that in such an instance as coming together to an entire familiarity and union of soul and body; oh! and this without being so much as well wishers to each other, but for increase of fortune.

PHIL.   But Madam, all these vexations will end very soon in one for all. Mr. Cimberton is your mother's kinsman, and three hundred years an older gentleman than any lover you ever had; for which reason, with that of his prodigious large estate, she is resolved on him, and has sent to consult the lawyers accordingly—nay, has (whether you know it or no) been in treaty with Sir Geoffry, who, to join in the settlement, has accepted of a sum to do it, and is every moment expected in town for that purpose.

LUC.   How do you get all this intelligence?

PHIL.   By an art I have, I thank my stars, beyond all the waiting-maids in Great Britain; the art of listening, Madam, for your ladyship's service.

LUC.   I shall soon know as much as you do. Leave me, leave me, Phillis, begone! Here, here, I'll turn you out. My mother says I must not converse with my servants, though I must converse with no one else.   (*Exit* PHILLIS)
How unhappy are we who are born to great fortunes! No one looks at us with indifference, or acts towards us on the foot of plain dealing; yet by all I have been heretofore offered to or treated for I have been used with the most agreeable of all abuses, flattery. But now, by this phlegmatic fool I am used as nothing, or a mere thing. He, forsooth! is too wise, too learned, to have any regard to desires, and I know not what the learned oaf calls sentiments of love and passion.—— Here he comes with my mother. It's much if he looks at me; or if he does, takes no more notice of me than of any other movable in the room.

Enter MRS. SEALAND *and* MR. CIMBERTON

MRS. SEAL.   How do I admire this noble, this learned taste of yours, and the worthy regard you have to our own ancient and honourable house, in consulting a means to keep the blood as pure and as regularly descended as may be.

CIMB.   Why, really, Madam, the young women of this age are treated with discourses of such a tendency, and their imaginations so bewildered in flesh and blood, that a man of reason can't talk to be understood. They have no ideas of happiness but what are more gross than the gratification of hunger and thirst.

LUC. (*aside*) With how much reflection he is a coxcomb!

CIMB. And in truth, Madam, I have considered it as a most brutal custom that persons of the first character in the world should go as ordinarily and with as little shame to bed as to dinner with one another. They proceed to the propagation of the species as openly as to the preservation of the individual.

LUC. (*aside*) She that willingly goes to bed to thee must have no shame, I'm sure.

MRS. SEAL. O Cousin Cimberton! Cousin Cimberton! how abstracted, how refined is your sense of things! But indeed, it is too true there is nothing so ordinary as to say, in the best governed families, "My master and lady are gone to bed"; one does not know but it might have been said of one's self.

(*hiding her face with her fan*)

CIMB. Lycurgus, Madam, instituted otherwise; among the Lacedæmonians the whole female world was pregnant, but none but the mothers themselves knew by whom. Their meetings were secret, and the amorous congress always by stealth, and no such professed doings between the sexes as are tolerated among us under the audacious word "marriage."

MRS. SEAL. Oh! had I lived in those days and been a matron of Sparta, one might with less indecency have had ten children, according to that modest institution, than one under the confusion of our modern, barefaced manner.

LUC. (*aside*) And yet, poor woman, she has gone through the whole ceremony, and here I stand a melancholy proof of it.

MRS. SEAL. We will talk then of business. That girl walking about the room there is to be your wife. She has, I confess, no ideas, no sentiments, that speak her born of a thinking mother.

CIMB. I have observed her; her lively look, free air, and disengaged countenance speak her very——

LUC. Very what?

CIMB. If you please, Madam——to set her a little that way.

MRS. SEAL. Lucinda, say nothing to him; you are not a match for him. When you are married, you may speak to such a husband when you're spoken to. But I am disposing of you above yourself every way.

CIMB. Madam, you cannot but observe the inconveniences I expose myself to, in hopes that your ladyship will be the consort of my better part. As for the young woman, she is rather an impediment than a help to a man of letters and speculation. Madam, there is no reflection, no philosophy, can at all times subdue the sensitive life, but the animal shall sometimes carry away the man. Ha! ay, the vermilion of her lips——

LUC. Pray, don't talk of me thus.

CIMB. The pretty enough—— Pant of her bosom——

LUC. Sir!—— Madam, don't you hear him?

CIMB.   Her forward chest——

LUC.   Intolerable!

CIMB.   High health——

LUC.   The grave, easy impudence of him!

CIMB.   Proud heart——

LUC.   Stupid coxcomb!

CIMB.   I say, Madam, her impatience while we are look-ing at her, throws out all attractions—her arms—her neck—what a spring in her step!

LUC.   Don't you run me over thus, you strange unaccount-able!

CIMB.   What an elasticity in her veins and arteries!

LUC.   I have no veins, no arteries.

MRS. SEAL.   O child, hear him; he talks finely; he's a scholar; he knows what you have.

CIMB.   The speaking invitation of her shape, the gathering of herself up, and the indignation you see in the pretty little thing. Now, I am considering her, on this occasion, but as one that is to be pregnant.

LUC. (*aside*)   The familiar, learned, unseasonable puppy!

CIMB.   And pregnant undoubtedly she will be yearly. I fear I shan't, for many years, have discretion enough to give her one fallow season.

LUC.   Monster! there's no bearing it. The hideous sot! there's no enduring it, to be thus surveyed like a steed at sale.

CIMB.   At sale! She's very illiterate—— But she's very well limbed too; turn her in; I see what she is.

(*Exit* LUCINDA, *in a rage*)

MRS. SEAL.   Go, you creature, I am ashamed of you.

CIMB.   No harm done.——You know, Madam, the better sort of people, as I observed to you, treat by their lawyers of weddings (*adjusting himself at the glass*) and the woman in the bargain, like the mansion-house in the sale of the estate, is thrown in, and what that is, whether good or bad, is not at all considered.

MRS. SEAL.   I grant it, and therefore make no demand for her youth and beauty, and every other accomplishment, as the common world think 'em, because she is not polite.

CIMB.   Madam, I know your exalted understanding, ab-stracted as it is from vulgar prejudices, will not be offended when I declare to you, I marry to have an heir to my estate, and not to beget a colony or a plantation. This young wom-an's beauty and constitution will demand provision for a tenth child at least.

MRS. SEAL (*aside*)   With all that wit and learning, how considerate! What an economist!—— Sir, I cannot make her any other than she is, or say she is much better than the other young women of this age, or fit for much besides being a mother; but I have given directions for the marriage settle-ments, and Sir Geoffry Cimberton's counsel is to meet ours here at this hour, concerning his joining in the deed which,

38

when executed, makes you capable of settling what is due to Lucinda's fortune. Herself, as I told you, I say nothing of.

CIMB. No, no, no, indeed, Madam, it is not usual; and I must depend upon my own reflection and philosophy not to overstock my family.

MRS. SEAL. I cannot help her, Cousin Cimberton, but she is, for aught I see, as well as the daughter of anybody else.

CIMB. That is very true, Madam.

Enter a Servant, who whispers MRS. SEALAND

MRS. SEAL. The lawyers are come, and now we are to hear what they have resolved as to the point whether it's necessary that Sir Geoffry should join in the settlement, as being what they call in the remainder. But, good Cousin, you must have patience with 'em. These lawyers, I am told, are of a different kind; one is what they call a chamber counsel, the other a pleader. The conveyancer is slow, from an imperfection in his speech, and therefore shunned the bar, but extremely passionate and impatient of contradiction. The other is as warm as he, but has a tongue so voluble, and a head so conceited, he will suffer nobody to speak but himself.

CIMB. You mean old Sergeant Target and Counsellor Bramble? I have heard of 'em.

MRS. SEAL. The same.—— Show in the gentlemen.

(Exit Servant)

Re-enter Servant, introducing MYRTLE *and*
TOM *disguised as* BRAMBLE *and* TARGET

MRS. SEAL. Gentlemen, this is the party concerned, Mr. Cimberton; and I hope you have considered of the matter.

TAR. Yes, Madam, we have agreed that it must be by indent-dent-dent-dent——

BRAM. Yes, Madam, Mr. Sergeant and myself have agreed, as he is pleased to inform you, that it must be an indenture tripartite, and tripartite let it be, for Sir Geoffry must needs be a party; old Cimberton, in the year 1619, says, in that ancient roll in Mr. Sergeant's hands, as, recourse thereto being had, will more at large appear——

TAR. Yes, and by the deeds in your hands, it appears that——

BRAM. Mr. Sergeant, I beg of you to make no inferences upon what is in our custody, but speak to the titles in your own deeds. I shall not show that deed till my client is in town.

CIMB. You know best your own methods.

MRS. SEAL. The single question is whether the entail is such that my cousin, Sir Geoffry, is necessary in this affair.

BRAM. Yes, as to the lordship of Tretriplet, but not as to the messuage of Grimgribber.

TAR. I say that Gr-Gr- that Gr-Gr-Grimgribber, Grimgribber is in us; that is to say, the remainder thereof, as well as that of Tr-Tr-triplet.

BRAM.   You go upon the deed of Sir Ralph, made in the middle of the last century, precedent to that in which old Cimberton made over the remainder, and made it pass to the heirs general, by which your client comes in; and I question whether the remainder even of Tretriplet is in him. But we are willing to waive that, and give him a valuable consideration. But we shall not purchase what is in us forever, as Grimgribber is, at the rate as we guard against the contingent of Mr. Cimberton having no son. Then we know Sir Geoffry is the first of the collateral male line in this family. Yet——

TAR.   Sir, Gr-Gr-ber is——

BRAM.   I apprehend you very well, and your argument might be of force, and we would be inclined to hear that in all its parts. But, Sir, I see very plain what you are going into. I tell you, it is as probable a contingent that Sir Geoffry may die before Mr. Cimberton, as that he may outlive him.

TAR.   Sir, we are not ripe for that yet, but I must say——

BRAM.   Sir, I allow you the whole extent of that argument; but that will go no farther than as to the claimants under old Cimberton. I am of opinion that, according to the instruction of Sir Ralph, he could not dock the entail and then create a new estate for the heirs general.

TAR.   Sir, I have not patience to be told that, when Gr-Gr-ber——

BRAM.   I will allow it you, Mr. Sergeant; but there must be the word "heirs for ever," to make such an estate as you pretend.

CIMB.   I must be impartial, though you are counsel for my side of the question. Were it not that you are so good as to allow him what he has not said, I should think it very hard you should answer him without hearing him. But, gentlemen, I believe you have both considered this matter and are firm in your different opinions. 'Twere better, therefore, you proceeded according to the particular sense of each of you and gave your thoughts distinctly in writing. And do you see, Sirs, pray let me have a copy of what you say, in English.

BRAM.   Why, what is all we have been saying? In English! Oh! but I forgot myself; you're a wit. But, however, to please you, Sir, you shall have it in as plain terms as the law will admit of.

CIMB.   But I would have it, Sir, without delay.

BRAM.   That, Sir, the law will not admit of: the courts are sitting at Westminster, and I am this moment obliged to be at every one of them, and 'twould be wrong if I should not be in the Hall to attend one of 'em at least; the rest would take it ill else. Therefore I must leave what I have said to Mr. Sergeant's consideration, and I will digest his arguments on my part, and you shall hear from me again, Sir.

(*Exit* BRAMBLE)

TAR.   Agreed, agreed.

40

CIMB. Mr. Bramble is very quick. He parted a little abruptly.

TAR. He could not bear my argument; I pinched him to the quick about that Gr-Gr-ber.

MRS. SEAL. I saw that, for he durst not so much as hear you. I shall send to you, Mr. Sergeant, as soon as Sir Geoffry comes to town, and then I hope all may be adjusted.

TAR. I shall be at my chambers at my usual hours.

(*Exit*)

CIMB. Madam, if you please, I'll now attend you to the tea table, where I shall hear from your ladyship reason and good sense, after all this law and gibberish.

MRS. SEAL. 'Tis a wonderful thing, Sir, that men of professions do not study to talk the substance of what they have to say in the language of the rest of the world. Sure, they'd find their account in it.

CIMB. They might, perhaps, Madam, with people of your good sense; but with the generality 'twould never do. The vulgar would have no respect for truth and knowledge if they were exposed to naked view.

Truth is too simple, of all art bereav'd:
Since the world will—why, let it be deceiv'd. (*Exeunt*)

ACT IV

SCENE I

SCENE: BEVIL JUNIOR's *lodgings*

BEVIL JUNIOR, *with a letter in his hand, followed by* TOM

TOM.   Upon my life, Sir, I know nothing of the matter. I never opened my lips to Mr. Myrtle about anything of your honour's letter to Madam Lucinda.

BEV. JUN.   What's the fool in such a fright for? I don't suppose you did. What I would know is, whether Mr. Myrtle showed any suspicion, or asked you any questions, to lead you to say casually that you had carried any such letter for me this morning.

TOM.   Why, Sir, if he did ask me any questions, how could I help it?

BEV. JUN.   I don't say you could, oaf! I am not questioning you, but him. What did he say to you?

TOM.   Why, Sir, when I came to his chambers, to be dressed for the lawyer's part your honour was pleased to put me upon, he asked me if I had been at Mr. Sealand's this morning. So I told him, Sir, I often went thither—because, Sir, if I had not said that, he might have thought there was something more in my going now than at another time.

BEV. JUN.   Very well!—— (*aside*)   The fellow's caution, I find, has given him this jealousy.—— Did he ask you no other questions?

TOM.   Yes, Sir; now I remember as we came away in the hackney coach from Mr. Sealand's, "Tom," says he, "as I came in to your master this morning, he bade you go for an answer to a letter he had sent. Pray, did you bring him any?" says he. "Ah!" says I, "Sir, your honour is pleased to joke with me; you have a mind to know whether I can keep a secret or no?"

BEV. JUN.   And so, by showing him you could, you told him you had one?

TOM. (*confused*)   Sir——

BEV. JUN.   What mean actions does jealousy make a man stoop to! How poorly has he used art with a servant to make him betray his own master!—— Well, and when did he give you this letter for me?

TOM.   Sir, he writ it before he pulled off his lawyer's gown, at his own chambers.

BEV. JUN.   Very well; and what did he say when you brought him my answer to it?

TOM.   He looked a little out of humour, Sir, and said it was very well.

BEV. JUN.   I knew he would be grave upon't. Wait without.

TOM.   Humh! 'gad, I don't like this; I am afraid we are all in the wrong box here.   (*Exit* TOM)

BEV. JUN.   I put on a serenity while my fellow was present; but I have never been more thoroughly disturbed. This hot man! to write me a challenge, on supposed artificial dealing, when I professed myself his friend! I can live contented without glory, but I cannot suffer shame. What's to be done? But first let me consider Lucinda's letter again.   (*reads*)

"SIR,

"I hope it is consistent with the laws a woman ought to impose upon herself, to acknowledge that your manner of declining a treaty of marriage in our family, and desiring the refusal may come from me, has something more engaging in it than the courtship of him who, I fear, will fall to my lot, except your friend exerts himself for our common safety and happiness. I have reasons for desiring Mr. Myrtle may not know of this letter till hereafter, and am your most obliged humble servant,

"Lucinda Sealand."

Well, but the postscript——   (*reads*)

"I won't, upon second thoughts, hide anything from you. But my reason for concealing this is that Mr. Myrtle has a jealousy in his temper which gives me some terrors; but my esteem for him inclines me to hope that only an ill effect which sometimes accompanies a tender love, and what may be cured by a careful and unblameable conduct."

Thus has this lady made me her friend and confidant, and put herself, in a kind, under my protection. I cannot tell him immediately the purport of her letter, except I could cure him of the violent and untractable passion of jealousy, and so serve him and her, by disobeying her in the article of secrecy, more than I should by complying with her directions. But then this duelling, which custom has imposed upon every man who would live with reputation and honour in the world——how must I preserve myself from imputations there? He'll, forsooth, call it or think it fear, if I explain without fighting. But his letter——I'll read it again——

"SIR,

"You have used me basely in corresponding and carrying on a treaty where you told me you were indifferent. I have changed my sword since I saw you, which advertisement I thought proper to send you against the next meeting between you and the injured

"Charles Myrtle."

TOM.   Mr. Myrtle, Sir. Would your honour please to see him?

BEV. JUN.   Why, you stupid creature! Let Mr. Myrtle wait at my lodgings? Show him up.   (*Exit* TOM)
Well! I am resolved upon my carriage to him. He is in love, and in every circumstance of life a little distrustful, which I must allow for—— but here he is.

Enter TOM, *introducing* MYRTLE

Sir, I am extremely obliged to you for this honour.—— But, Sir, you, with your very discerning face, leave the room.
                    (*Exit* TOM)

Well, Mr. Myrtle, your commands with me?

MYRT.   The time, the place, our long acquaintance, and many other circumstances which affect me on this occasion, oblige me, without farther ceremony or conference, to desire you would not only, as you already have, acknowledge the receipt of my letter, but also comply with the request in it. I must have farther notice taken of my message than these half lines—— "I have yours—I shall be at home."

BEV. JUN.   Sir, I own I have received a letter from you in a very unusual style; but as I design everything in this matter shall be your own action, your own seeking, I shall understand nothing but what you are pleased to confirm face to face, and I have already forgot the contents of your epistle.

MYRT.   This cool manner is very agreeable to the abuse you have already made of my simplicity and frankness, and I see your moderation tends to your own advantage and not mine; to your own safety, not consideration of your friend.

BEV. JUN.   My own safety, Mr. Myrtle?

MYRT.   Your own safety, Mr. Bevil.

BEV. JUN.   Look you, Mr. Myrtle, there's no disguising that I understand what you would be at; but, Sir, you know I have often daréd to disapprove of the decisions a tryant custom has introduced, to the breach of all laws, both divine and human.

MYRT.   Mr. Bevii, Mr. Bevil, it would be a good first principle in those who have so tender a conscience that way, to have as much abhorrence of doing injuries as——

BEV. JUN.   As what?

MYRT.   As fear of answering for 'em.

BEV. JUN.   As fear of answering for 'em! But that apprehension is just or blameable according to the object of that fear. I have often told you, in confidence of heart, I abhorred the daring to offend the Author of life, and rushing into His presence—I say, by the very same act, to commit the crime against Him, and immediately to urge on to His tribunal.

MYRT.   Mr. Bevil, I must tell you, this coolness, this gravity, this show of conscience, shall never cheat me of my mistress. You have, indeed, the best excuse for life—the hopes of possessing Lucinda. But consider, Sir, I have as much reason to be weary of it, if I am to lose her; and my first attempt to recover her shall be to let her see the dauntless man who is to be her guardian and protector.

BEV. JUN.   Sir, show me but the least glimpse of argument that I am authorized by my own hand to vindicate any lawless insult of this nature, and I will show thee, to chastise thee hardly deserves the name of courage—slight, inconsiderate man! There is, Mr. Myrtle, no such terror in quick anger; and you shall, you know not why, be cool, as you have, you know not why, been warm.

MYRT.   Is the woman one loves so little an occasion of anger? You, perhaps, who know not what it is to love, who have your ready, your commodious, your foreign trinket for your loose hours, and from your fortune, your specious outward carriage, and other lucky circumstances, as easy a way to the possession of a woman of honour—you know nothing of what it is to be alarmed, to be distracted with anxiety and terror of losing more than life. Your marriage, happy man! goes on like common business, and in the interim you have your rambling captive, your Indian princess, for your soft moments of dalliance—your convenient, your ready Indiana.

BEV. JUN.   You have touched me beyond the patience of a man, and I'm excusable, in the guard of innocence (or from the infirmity of human nature, which can bear no more), to accept your invitation and observe your letter. Sir, I'll attend you.

Enter TOM

TOM.   Did you call, Sir? I thought you did: I heard you speak aloud.

BEV. JUN.   Yes; go call a coach.

TOM.   Sir—master—Mr. Myrtle—friends—gentleman—what d'ye mean? I am but a servant, or——

BEV. JUN.   Call a coach!   (Exit TOM)

(a long pause, walking sullenly by each other) (aside) Shall I (though provoked to the uttermost) recover myself at the entrance of a third person, and that my servant, too, and not have respect enough to all I have ever been receiving from infancy, the obligation to the best of fathers, to an unhappy virgin too, whose life depends on mine? (shutting the door—— to MYRTLE) I have, thank heaven, had time to recollect myself, and shall not, for fear of what such a rash man as you think of me, keep longer unexplained the false appearances under which your infirmity of temper makes you suffer, when perhaps too much regard to a false point of honour makes me prolong that suffering.

MYRT.   I am sure Mr. Bevil cannot doubt but I had rather have satisfaction from his innocence than his sword.

BEV. JUN.   Why, then, would you ask it first that way?

MYRT.   Consider, you kept your temper yourself no longer

45

than till I spoke to the disadvantage of her you loved.

BEV. JUN.   True; but let me tell you, I have saved you from the most exquisite distress, even though you had succeeded in the dispute. I know you so well that I am sure to have found this letter about a man you had killed would have been worse than death to yourself. Read it.—(*aside*)   When he is thoroughly mortified and shame has got the better of jealousy, when he has seen himself throughly, he will deserve to be assisted towards obtaining Lucinda.

MYRT.   (*aside*)   With what a superiority has he turned the injury on me, as the aggressor! I begin to fear I have been too far transported. "A treaty in our family" is not that saying too much? I shall relapse. But I find (on the postscript) "something like jealousy." With what face can I see my benefactor, my advocate, whom I have treated like a betrayer?—— Oh! Bevil, with what words shall I——

BEV. JUN.   There needs none; to convince is much more than to conquer.

MYRT.   But can you——

BEV. JUN.   You have o'erpaid the inquietude you gave me, in the change I see in you towards me. Alas! what machines are we! Thy face is altered to that of another man—to that of my companion, my friend.

MYRT.   That I could be such a precipitant wretch!

BEV. JUN.   Pray, no more!

MYRT.   Let me reflect how many friends have died by the hands of friends, for want of temper; and you must give me leave to say again and again how much I am beholden to that superior spirit you have subdued me with. What had become of one of us, or perhaps both, had you been as weak as I was, and as incapable of reason?   ·

BEV. JUN.   I congratulate to us both the escape from ourselves, and hope the memory of it will make us dearer friends than ever.

MYRT.   Dear Bevil, your friendly conduct has convinced me that there is nothing manly but what is conducted by reason and agreeable to the practice of virtue and justice. And yet how many have been sacrificed to that idol, the unreasonable opinion of men! Nay, they are so ridiculous, in it, that they often use their swords against each other with dissembled anger and real fear.

Betray'd by honour and compell'd by shame,
They hazard being to preserve a name:
Nor dare enquire into the dread mistake,
Till plung'd in sad eternity they wake.   (*Exeunt*)

SCENE: *St. James's Park*

Enter SIR JOHN BEVIL *and* MR. SEALAND

SIR J. BEV. Give me leave, however, Mr. Sealand, as we are upon a treaty for uniting our families, to mention only the business of an ancient house. Genealogy and descent are to be of some consideration in an affair of this sort.

MR. SEAL. Genealogy and descent! Sir, there has been in our family a very large one. There was Galfrid the father of Edward, the father of Ptolemy, the father of Crassus, the father of Earl Richard, the father of Henry the Marquis, the father of Duke John——

SIR J. BEV. What, do you rave, Mr. Sealand?—— all these great names in your family?

MR. SEAL. These? Yes, Sir. I have heard my father name 'em all, and more.

SIR J. BEV. Ay, Sir? and did he say they were all in your family?

MR. SEAL. Yes, Sir, he kept 'em all. He was the greatest cocker in England. He said Duke John won him many battles, and never lost one.

SIR J. BEV. Oh, Sir, your servant! you are laughing at my laying any stress upon descent; but I must tell you, Sir, I never knew anyone but he that wanted that advantage turn it into ridicule.

MR. SEAL. And I never knew anyone who had many better advantages put that into his account. But, Sir John, value yourself as you please upon your ancient house, I am to talk freely of everything you are pleased to put into your bill of rates on this occasion. Yet, Sir, I have made no objections to your son's family. 'Tis his morals that I doubt.

SIR J. BEV. Sir, I can't help saying that what might injure a citizen's credit may be no stain to a gentleman's honour.

MR. SEAL. Sir John, the honour of a gentleman is liable to be tainted by as small a matter as the credit of a trader. We are talking of a marriage, and in such a case the father of a young woman will not think it an addition to the honour or credit of her lover that he is a keeper——

SIR J. BEV. Mr. Sealand, don't take upon you to spoil my son's marriage with any woman else.

MR. SEAL. Sir John, let him apply to any woman else, and have as many mistresses as he pleases.

SIR J. BEV. My son, Sir, is a discreet and sober gentleman.

MR. SEAL. Sir, I never saw a man that wenched soberly and discreetly that ever left it off; the decency observed in the practice hides, even from the sinner, the iniquity of it. They pursue it, not that their appetites hurry 'em away, but, I warrant you, because 'tis their opinion they may do it.

SIR J. BEV. Were what you suspect a truth—— do you

design to keep your daughter a virgin till you find a man unblemished that way?

MR. SEAL. Sir, as much a cit as you take me for, I know the town and the world—and give me leave to say that we merchants are a species of gentry that have grown into the world this last century, and are as honourable, and almost as useful, as you landed folks that have always thought yourselves so much above us; for your trading, forsooth! is extended no farther than a load of hay or a fat ox. You are pleasant people, indeed, because you are generally bred up to be lazy; therefore, I warrant you, industry is dishonourable.

SIR J. BEV. Be not offended, Sir; let us go back to our point.

MR. SEAL. Oh, not at all offended! but I don't love to leave any part of the account unclosed; look you, Sir John, comparisons are odious, and more particularly so on occasions of this kind, when we are projecting races that are to be made out of both sides of the comparisons.

SIR J. BEV. But my son, Sir, is, in the eye of the world, a gentleman of merit.

MR. SEAL. I own to you, I think him so. But, Sir John, I am a man exercised and experienced in chances and disasters. I lost, in my earlier years, a very fine wife, and with her a poor little infant; this makes me, perhaps, overcautious to preserve the second bounty of Providence to me, and be as careful as I can of this child. You'll pardon me; my poor girl, Sir, is as valuable to me as your boasted son to you.

SIR J. BEV. Why, that's one very good reason, Mr. Sealand, why I wish my son had her.

MR. SEAL. There is nothing but this strange lady here, this *incognita*, that can be objected to him. Here and there a man falls in love with an artful creature, and gives up all the motives of life to that one passion.

SIR J. BEV. A man of my son's understanding cannot be supposed to be one of them.

MR. SEAL. Very wise men have been so enslaved, and when a man marries with one of them upon his hands, whether moved from the demand of the world or slighter reasons, such a husband soils with his wife for a month perhaps—then "Good b'w'ye, Madam!"—the show's over. Ah! John Dryden points out such a husband to a hair, where he says,

> And while abroad so prodigal the dolt is,
> Poor spouse at home as ragged as a colt is.

Now, in plain terms, Sir, I shall not care to have my poor girl turned a-grazing, and that must be the case when——

SIR J. BEV. But pray consider, Sir, my son——

MR. SEAL. Look you, Sir, I'll make the matter short. This unknown lady, as I told you, is all the objection I have to him; but, one way or other, he is, or has been, certainly engaged to her. I am therefore resolved this very afternoon to visit her. Now, from her behaviour or appearance I shall soon be let into what I may fear or hope for.

SIR J. BEV. Sir, I am very confident there can be nothing enquired into, relating to my son, that will not, upon being understood, turn to his advantage.

MR. SEAL. I hope that as sincerely as you believe it. Sir John Bevil, when I am satisfied in this great point, if your son's conduct answers the character you give him, I shall wish your alliance more than that of any gentleman in Great Britain—and so, your servant!   (*Exit*)

SIR J. BEV. He is gone in a way but barely civil; but his great wealth, and the merit of his only child, the heiress of it, are not to be lost for a little peevishness.

Enter HUMPHREY

Oh, Humphrey! you are come in a seasonable minute. I want to talk to thee, and to tell thee that my head and heart are on the rack about my son.

HUMPH. Sir, you may trust his discretion; I am sure you may.

SIR J. BEV. Why, I do believe I may, and yet I'm in a thousand fears when I lay this vast wealth before me. When I consider his prepossessions, either generous to a folly in an honourable love, or abandoned past redemption in a vicious one; and, from the one or the other, his insensibility to the fairest prospect towards doubling our estate: a father who knows how useful wealth is, and how necessary, even to those who despise it—I say a father, Humphrey, a father cannot bear it.

HUMPH. Be not transported, Sir; you will grow incapable of taking any resolution in your perplexity.

SIR J. BEV. Yet, as angry as I am with him, I would not have him surprised in anything. This mercantile rough man may go grossly into the examination of this matter, and talk to the gentlewoman so as to——

HUMPH. No, I hope, not in an abrupt manner.

SIR J. BEV. No, I hope not! Why, dost thou know anything of her, or of him, or of anything of it, or all of it?

HUMPH. My dear master, I know so much that I told him this very day you had reason to be secretly out of humour about her.

SIR J. BEV. Did you go so far? Well, what said he to that?

HUMPH. His words were, looking upon me steadfastly: "Humphrey," says he, "that woman is a woman of honour."

SIR J. BEV. How! Do you think he is married to her, or designs to marry her?

HUMPH. I can say nothing to the latter, but he says he can marry no one without your consent while you are living.

SIR J. BEV. If he said so much, I know he scorns to break his word with me.

HUMPH.   I am sure of that.

SIR J. BEV.   You are sure of that. Well! that's some comfort. Then I have nothing to do but to see the bottom of this
matter during this present ruffle.—O Humphrey——

HUMPH.   You are not ill, I hope, Sir.

SIR J. BEV.   Yes, a man is very ill that's in a very ill humour.
To be a father is to be in care for one whom you oftener disoblige than please by that very care. Oh, that sons could
know the duty to a father before they themselves are fathers!
But perhaps you'll say now that I am one of the happiest
fathers in the world; but I assure you, that of the very happiest is not a condition to be envied.

HUMPH.   Sir, your pain arises, not from the thing itself,
but your particular sense of it. You are overfond—nay, give
me leave to say you are unjustly apprehensive from your
fondness. My master Bevil never disobliged you, and he will
—I know he will—do everything you ought to expect.

SIR J. BEV.   He won't take all this money with this girl.
For aught I know, he will, forsooth, have so much moderation as to think he ought not to force his liking for any consideration.

HUMPH.   He is to marry her, not you; he is to live with
her, not you, Sir.

SIR J. BEV.   I know not what to think. But I know nothing
can be more miserable than to be in this doubt. Follow me;
I must come to some resolution.   (*Exeunt*)

SCENE III

SCENE: BEVIL JUNIOR'S *lodgings*

Enter TOM *and* PHILLIS

TOM.   Well, Madam, if you must speak with Mr. Myrtle,
you shall; he is now with my master in the library.

PHIL.   But you must leave me alone with him, for he can't
make me a present, nor I so handsomely take anything from
him, before you: it would not be decent.

TOM.   It will be very decent, indeed, for me to retire and
leave my mistress with another man.

PHIL.   He is a gentleman and will treat one properly.

TOM.   I believe so; but, however, I won't be far off, and
therefore will venture to trust you. I'll call him to you.

                                             (*Exit* TOM)

PHIL.   What a deal of pother and sputter here is between
my mistress and Mr. Myrtle from mere punctilio! I could, any
hour of the day, get her to her lover, and would do it—but
she, forsooth, will allow no plot to get him; but, if he can
come to her, I know she would be glad of it. I must, therefore, do her an acceptable violence and surprise her into his
arms. I am sure I go by the best rule imaginable. If she were
my maid, I should think her the best servant in the world for
doing so by me.

Oh, Sir! You and Mr. Bevil are fine gentlemen to let a lady remain under such difficulties as my poor mistress, and no attempt to set her at liberty or release her from the danger of being instantly married to Cimberton.

MYRT. Tom has been telling—— but what is to be done?

PHIL. What is to be done—when a man can't come at his mistress! Why, can't you fire our house, or the next house to us, to make us run out, and you take us?

MYRT. How, Mrs. Phillis!

PHIL. Ay; let me see that rogue deny to fire a house, make a riot, or any other little thing, when there were no other way to come at me.

TOM. I am obliged to you, Madam.

PHIL. Why, don't we hear every day of people's hanging themselves for love, and won't they venture the hazard of being hanged for love? Oh! were I a man——

MYRT. What manly thing would you have me undertake, according to your ladyship's notion of a man?

PHIL. Only be at once what, one time or other, you may be, and wish to be, or must be.

MYRT. Dear girl, talk plainly to me, and consider I, in my condition, can't be in very good humour. You say, to be at once what I must be.

PHIL. Ay, ay—I mean no more than to be an old man; I saw you do it very well at the masquerade. In a word, old Sir Geoffry Cimberton is every hour expected in town to join in the deeds and settlements for marrying Mr. Cimberton. He is half blind, half lame, half deaf, half dumb; though as to his passions and desires he is as warm and ridiculous as when in the heat of youth.

TOM. Come to the business, and don't keep the gentleman in suspense for the pleasure of being courted, as you serve me.

PHIL. I saw you at the masquerade act such a one to perfection. Go and put on that very habit, and come to our house as Sir Geoffry. There is not one there but myself knows his person; I was born in the parish where he is lord of the manor. I have seen him often and often at church in the country. Do not hesitate, but come thither; they will think you bring a certain security against Mr. Myrtle, and you bring Mr. Myrtle! Leave the rest to me. I leave this with you, and expect—— They don't, I told you, know you; they think you out of town, which you had as good be for ever if you lose this opportunity. I must be gone; I know I am wanted at home.

MYRT. My dear Phillis!

(*catches and kisses her, and gives her money*)

PHIL. O fie! my kisses are not my own; you have committed violence; but I'll carry 'em to the right owner. (TOM *kisses her—To* TOM) Come, see me downstairs, and leave

51

the lover to think of his last game for the prize.

(*Exeunt* TOM *and* PHILLIS)

MYRT.   I think I will instantly attempt this wild expedient.

The extravagance of it will make me less suspected, and it will give me opportunity to assert my own right to Lucinda, without whom I cannot live. But I am so mortified at this conduct of mine towards poor Bevil. He must think meanly of me. I know not how to reassume myself and be in spirit enough for such an adventure as this. Yet I must attempt it, if it be only to be near Lucinda under her present perplexities; and sure—

The next delight to transport with the fair,
Is to relieve her in her hours of care.   (*Exit*)

ACT V

SCENE I

SCENE: SEALAND'S *house*

Enter PHILLIS, *with lights, before* MYRTLE, *disguised like old*
SIR GEOFFRY, *supported by* MRS. SEALAND, LUCINDA, *and*
CIMBERTON

MRS. SEAL.   Now I have seen you thus far, Sir Geoffry,
will you excuse me a moment while I give my necessary
orders for your accommodation?   (*Exit* MRS. SEALAND)

MYRT.   I have not seen you, Cousin Cimberton, since you
were ten years old; and as it is incumbent on you to keep
up our name and family, I shall, upon very reasonable terms,
join with you in a settlement to that purpose. Though I must
tell you, Cousin, this is the first merchant that has married
into our house.

LUC. (*aside*)   Deuce on 'em! am I a merchant because my
father is?

MYRT.   But is he directly a trader at this time?

CIMB.   There's no hiding the disgrace, Sir; he trades to
all parts of the world.

MYRT.   We never had one of our family before who descended from persons that did anything.

CIMB.   Sir, since it is a girl that they have, I am, for the
honour of my family, willing to take it in again, and to sink
her into our name, and no harm done.

MYRT.   'Tis prudently and generously resolved. Is this the
young thing?

CIMB.   Yes, Sir.

PHIL. (*to* LUCINDA)   Good Madam, don't be out of humour, but let them run to the utmost of their extravagance.
Hear them out.

MYRT.   Can't I see her nearer? My eyes are but weak.

PHIL. (*to* LUCINDA)   Beside, I am sure the uncle has something worth your notice. I'll take care to get off the young
one, and leave you to observe what may be wrought out of
the old one for your good.   (*Exit*)

CIMB.   Madam, this old gentleman, your great-uncle, desires to be introduced to you and to see you nearer—— Approach, Sir.

MYRT.   By your leave, young lady. (*puts on spectacles*)

——Cousin Cimberton! She has exactly that sort of neck and bosom for which my sister Gertrude was so much admired in the year sixty-one, before the French dresses first discovered anything in women below the chin.

LUC. (*aside*) What a very odd situation am I in!—though I cannot but be diverted at the extravagance of their humours, equally unsuitable to their age.—— Chin, quotha! I don't believe my passionate lover there knows whether I have one or not. Ha! ha!

MYRT. Madam, I would not willingly offend, but I have a better glass—— (*pulls out a large one*)

Enter PHILLIS *to* CIMBERTON

PHIL. Sir, my lady desires to show the apartment to you that she intends for Sir Geoffry.

CIMB. Well, Sir, by that time you have sufficiently gazed and sunned yourself in the beauties of my spouse there, I will wait on you again. (*Exeunt* CIMBERTON *and* PHYLLIS)

MYRT. Were it not, Madam, that I might be troublesome, there is something of importance, though we are alone, which I would say more safe from being heard.

LUC. There is something in this old fellow, methinks, that raises my curiosity.

MYRT. To be free, Madam, I as heartily contemn this kinsman of mine as you do, and am sorry to see so much beauty and merit devoted by your parents to so insensible a possessor.

LUC. Surprising!——I hope, then, Sir, you will not contribute to the wrong you are so generous as to pity, whatever may be the interest of your family.

MYRT. This hand of mine shall never be employed to sign anything against your good and happiness.

LUC. I am sorry, Sir, it is not in my power to make you proper acknowledgments, but there is a gentleman in the world whose gratitude will, I am sure, be worthy of the favour.

MYRT. All the thanks I desire, Madam, are in your power to give.

LUC. Name them, and command them.

MYRT. Only, Madam, that the first time you are alone with your lover you will with open arms receive him.

LUC. As willingly as his heart could wish it.

MYRT. Thus, then, he claims your promise.—— O Lucinda!

LUC. Oh! a cheat! a cheat! a cheat!

MYRT. Hush! 'tis I, 'tis I, your lover, Myrtle himself, Madam.

LUC. Oh, bless me! what a rashness and folly to surprise me so—— But hush—— my mother.

Enter MRS. SEALAND, CIMBERTON, *and* PHILLIS

54

MRS. SEAL. How now! what's the matter?

LUC. O Madam! as soon as you left the room my uncle fell into a sudden fit, and—and—so I cried out for help to support him and conduct him to his chamber.

MRS. SEAL. That was kindly done. Alas, Sir! how do you find yourself?

MYRT. Never was taken in so odd a way in my life— pray, lead me! Oh! I was talking here—pray carry me—to my Cousin Cimberton's young lady——

MRS. SEAL. (aside) My Cousin Cimberton's young lady! How zealous he is, even in his extremity, for the match! a right Cimberton.

(CIMBERTON and LUCINDA lead him as one in pain, etc.)

CIMB. Pox! Uncle, you will pull my ear off.

LUC. Pray, Uncle! you will squeeze me to death.

MRS. SEAL. No matter, no matter—he knows not what he does. Come, Sir, shall I help you out?

MYRT. By no means! I'll trouble nobody but my young cousins here. (They lead him off)

PHIL. But pray, Madam, does your ladyship intend that Mr. Cimberton shall really marry my young mistress at last? I don't think he likes her.

MRS. SEAL. That's not material! Men of his speculation are above desires. But be it as it may, now I have given old Sir Geoffry the trouble of coming up to sign and seal, with what countenance can I be off?

PHIL. As well as with twenty others, Madam. It is the glory and honour of a great fortune to live in continual treaties, and still to break off: it looks great, Madam.

MRS. SEAL. True, Phillis—yet to return our blood again into the Cimbertons' is an honour not to be rejected. But were not you saying that Sir John Bevil's creature, Humphrey, has been with Mr. Sealand?

PHIL. Yes, Madam; I overheard them agree that Mr. Sealand should go himself and visit this unknown lady that Mr. Bevil is so great with; and if he found nothing there to fright him, that Mr. Bevil should still marry my young mistress.

MRS. SEAL. How! nay, then, he shall find she is my daughter as well as his. I'll follow him this instant and take the whole family along with me. The disputed power of disposing of my own daughter shall be at an end this very night. I'll live no longer in anxiety for a little hussy that hurts my appearance wherever I carry her, and for whose sake I seem to be not at all regarded, and that in the best of my days.

PHIL. Indeed, Madam, if she were married, your ladyship might very well be taken for Mr. Sealand's daughter.

MRS. SEAL. Nay, when the chit has not been with me, I have heard the men say as much. I'll no longer cut off the greatest pleasure of a woman's life—the shining in assemblies —by her forward anticipation of the respect that's due to her superior. She shall down to Cimberton Hall—she shall—she shall!

PHIL. I hope, Madam, I shall stay with your ladyship.

MRS. SEAL. Thou shalt, Phillis, and I'll place thee then more about me. But order chairs immediately—I'll be gone this minute. (*Exeunt*)

SCENE II

SCENE: Charing Cross

Enter MR. SEALAND and HUMPHREY

MR. SEAL. I am very glad, Mr. Humphrey, that you agree with me that it is for our common good I should look thoroughly into this matter.

HUMPH. I am, indeed, of that opinion; for there is no artifice, nothing concealed, in our family, which ought in justice to be known. I need not desire you, Sir, to treat the lady with care and respect.

MR. SEAL. Master Humphrey, I shall not be rude, though I design to be a little abrupt and come into the matter at once, to see how she will bear upon a surprise.

HUMPH. That's the door, Sir; I wish you success.—(*While* HUMPHREY *speaks* SEALAND *consults his table book*.) I am less concerned what happens there because I hear Mr. Myrtle is well lodged as old Sir Geoffry; so I am willing to let this gentleman employ himself here, to give them time at home: for I am sure 'tis necessary for the quiet of our family Lucinda were disposed of out of it, since Mr. Bevil's inclination is so much otherwise engaged. (*Exit*)

MR. SEAL. I think this is the door. (*knocks*) I'll carry this matter with an air of authority, to enquire, though I make an errand to begin discourse. (*knocks again, and enter a Foot-boy*) So, young man! is your lady within?

BOY. Alack, Sir! I am but a country boy—I dan't know whether she is or noa; but an you'll stay a bit, I'll goa and ask the gentlewoman that's with her.

MR. SEAL. Why, Sirrah, though you are a country boy, you can see, can't you? you know whether she is at home, when you see her, don't you?

BOY. Nay, nay, I'm not such a country lad neither, master, to think she's at home because I see her. I have been in town but a month, and I lost one place already for believing my own eyes.

MR. SEAL. Why, Sirrah! have you learnt to lie already?

BOY. Ah, master! things that are lies in the country are not lies at London—I begin to know my business a little better than so. But an you please to walk in, I'll call a gentlewoman to you that can tell you for certain—she can make bold to ask my lady herself.

MR. SEAL. Oh! then she is within, I find, though you dare

not say so.

BOY. Nay, nay! that's neither here nor there: what's matter whether she is within or no, if she has not a mind to see anybody?

MR. SEAL. I can't tell, Sirrah, whether you are arch or simple; but, however, get me a direct answer, and here's a shilling for you.

BOY. Will you please to walk in; I'll see what I can do for you.

MR. SEAL. I see you will be fit for your business in time, child. But I expect to meet with nothing but extraordinaries in such a house.

BOY. Such a house! Sir, you han't seen it yet. Pray walk in.

MR. SEAL. Sir, I'll wait upon you.   (*Exeunt*)

SCENE III

SCENE: INDIANA'S *house*

Enter ISABELLA

ISAB. What anxiety do I feel for this poor creature! What will be the end of her? Such a languishing, unreserved passion for a man that at last must certainly leave or ruin her—and perhaps both! Then the aggravation of the distress is, that she does not believe he will—not but, I must own, if they are both what they would seem, they are made for one another as much as Adam and Eve were, for there is no other of their kind but themselves.

Enter Boy

So, Daniel! what news with you?

BOY. Madam, there's a gentleman below would speak with my lady.

ISAB. Sirrah! don't you know Mr. Bevil yet?

BOY. Madam, 'tis not the gentleman who comes every day, and asks for you, and won't go in till he knows whether you are with her or no.

JSAB. Ha! that's a particular I did not know before.—— Well, be it who it will, let him come up to me.

(*Exit Boy, and re-enters with* MR. SEALAND; ISABELLA *looks amazed*)

MR. SEAL. Madam, I can't blame your being a little surprised to see a perfect stranger make a visit, and——

ISAB. I am indeed surprised!—— (*aside*) I see he does not know me.

MR. SEAL. You are very prettily lodged here, Madam; in troth, you seem to have everything in plenty.—— (*aside, and looking about*) A thousand a year, I warrant you, upon this pretty nest of rooms and the dainty one within them.

ISAB. (*apart*) Twenty years, it seems, have less effect in

the alteration of a man of thirty than of a girl of fourteen—
he's almost still the same. But alas! I find by other men, as
well as himself, I am not what I was. As soon as he spoke I
was convinced 'twas he. How shall I contain my surprise and
satisfaction! he must not know me yet.

MR. SEAL. Madam, I hope I don't give you any disturb-
ance, but there is a young lady here with whom I have a
particular business to discourse, and I hope she will admit
me to that favour.

ISAB. Why, Sir, have you had any notice concerning her?
I wonder who could give it you.

MR. SEAL. That, Madam, is fit only to be communicated
to herself.

ISAB. Well, Sir! you shall see her.—— (*aside*) I find he
knows nothing yet, nor shall from me. I am resolved I will
observe this interlude, this sport of nature and of fortune.——
You shall see her presently, Sir, for now I am as a mother,
and will trust her with you.   (*Exit*)

MR. SEAL. As a mother! right; that's the old phrase for
one of those commode ladies, who lend out beauty for hire
to young gentlemen that have pressing occasions. But here
comes the precious lady herself. In troth, a very sightly
woman!

Enter INDIANA

IND. I am told, Sir, you have some affair that requires
your speaking with me.

MR. SEAL. Yes, Madam: there came to my hands a bill
drawn by Mr. Bevil, which is payable to-morrow, and he, in
the intercourse of business, sent it to me, who have cash of
his, and desired me to send a servant with it; but I have
made bold to bring you the money myself.

IND. Sir! was that necessary?

MR. SEAL. No, Madam; but, to be free with you, the fame
of your beauty and the regard which Mr. Bevil is a little too
well known to have for you, excited my curiosity.

IND. Too well known to have for me! Your sober appearance, Sir, which my friend described, made me expect no
rudeness, or absurdity, at least.—— Who's there?—— Sir, if
you pay the money to a servant 'twill be as well.

MR. SEAL. Pray, Madam, be not offended. I came hither on
an innocent, nay, a virtuous design; and if you will have
patience to hear me it may be as useful to you, as you are in
a friendship with Mr. Bevil, as to my only daughter, whom
I was this day disposing of.

IND. You make me hope, Sir, I have mistaken you. I am
composed again; be free, say on—— (*aside*) what I am afraid
to hear.

MR. SEAL. I feared, indeed, an unwarranted passion here,
but I did not think it was in abuse of so worthy an object,
so accomplished a lady as your sense and mien bespeak. But

the youth of our age care not what merit and virtue they bring to shame, so they gratify——

IND. Sir, you are going into very great errors; but as you are pleased to say you see something in me that has changed at least the colour of your suspicions, so has your appearance altered mine, and made me earnestly attentive to what has any way concerned you to enquire into my affairs and character.

MR. SEAL. (*aside*) How sensibly, with what an air she talks!

IND. Good Sir, be seated, and tell me tenderly—keep all your suspicions concerning me alive, that you may in a proper and prepared way acquaint me why the care of your daughter obliges a person of your seeming worth and fortune to be thus inquisitive about a wretched, helpless, friendless—— (*weeping*). But I beg your pardon: though I am an orphan, your child is not; and your concern for her, it seems, has brought you hither. I'll be composed; pray go on, Sir.

MR. SEAL. How could Mr. Bevil be such a monster, to injure such a woman?

IND. No, Sir, you wrong him; he has not injured me; my support is from his bounty.

MR. SEAL. Bounty! when gluttons give high prices for delicates, they are prodigious bountiful!

IND. Still, still you will persist in that error. But my own fears tell me all. You are the gentleman, I suppose, for whose happy daughter he is designed a husband by his good father, and he has, perhaps, consented to the overture. He was here this morning, dressed beyond his usual plainness—nay, most sumptuously—and he is to be, perhaps, this night a bridegroom.

MR. SEAL. I own he was intended such; but, Madam, on your account, I have determined to defer my daughter's marriage till I am satisfied from your own mouth of what nature are the obligations you are under to him.

IND. His actions, Sir, his eyes, have only made me think he designed to make me the partner of his heart. The goodness and gentleness of his demeanour made me misinterpret all. 'Twas my own hope, my own passion, that deluded me; he never made one amorous advance to me. His large heart and bestowing hand have only helped the miserable. Nor know I why, but from his mere delight in virtue, that I have been his care, the object on which to indulge and please himself with pouring favours.

MR. SEAL. Madam, I know not why it is, but I, as well as you, am methinks afraid of entering into the matter I came about; but 'tis the same thing as if we had talked never so distinctly: he ne'er shall have a daughter of mine.

IND. If you say this from what you think of me, you wrong yourself and him. Let not me, miserable though I may be, do injury to my benefactor. No, Sir, my treatment ought rather to reconcile you to his virtues. If to bestow without a prospect of return; if to delight in supporting what might, perhaps, be thought an object of desire, with no other view than to be her guard against those who would not be so disinterested—if these actions, Sir, can in a careful parent's eye commend him to a daughter, give yours, Sir, give her to my honest, generous Bevil. What have I to do but sigh and weep, to rave, run wild, a lunatic in chains, or, hid in darkness, mutter in distracted starts and broken accents my strange, strange story!

MR. SEAL.   Take comfort, Madam.

IND.   All my comfort must be to expostulate in madness, to relieve with frenzy my despair, and shrieking to demand of fate, "Why—why was I born to such variety of sorrows?"

MR. SEAL.   If I have been the least occasion——

IND.   No, 'twas heaven's high will I should be such—to be plundered in my cradle! tossed on the seas! and even there an infant captive! to lose my mother, hear but of my father! to be adopted! lose my adopter! then plunged again in worse calamities!

MR. SEAL.   An infant captive!

IND.   Yet then to find the most charming of mankind, once more to set me free from what I thought the last distress; to load me with his services, his bounties and his favours; to support my very life in a way that stole, at the same time, my very soul itself from me!

MR. SEAL.   And has young Bevil been this worthy man?

IND.   Yet then, again, this very man to take another! without leaving me the right, the pretence, of easing my fond heart with tears! For, oh! I can't reproach him, though the same hand that raised me to this height now throws me down the precipice.

MR. SEAL.   Dear lady! Oh, yet one moment's patience: my heart grows full with your affliction. But yet there's something in your story that——

IND.   My portion here is bitterness and sorrow.

MR. SEAL.   Do not think so. Pray answer me: does Bevil know your name and family?

IND.   Alas, too well! Oh, could I be any other thing than what I am! I'll tear away all traces of my former self, my little ornaments, the remains of my first state, the hints of what I ought to have been——

(*In her disorder she throws away a bracelet, which* SEALAND *takes up, and looks earnestly on it.*)

MR. SEAL.   Ha! what's this? My eyes are not deceived? It is, it is the same! the very bracelet which I bequeathed my wife at our last mournful parting!

IND.   What said you, Sir! Your wife! Whither does my fancy carry me? What means this unfelt motion at my heart? And yet again my fortune but deludes me; for if I err not, Sir, your name is Sealand, but my lost father's name was——

60

MR. SEAL.   Danvers! was it not?

IND.   What new amazement! That is, indeed, my family.

MR. SEAL.   Know, then, when my misfortunes drove me to the Indies, for reasons too tedious now to mention, I changed my name of Danvers into Sealand.

Enter ISABELLA

ISAB.   If yet there wants an explanation of your wonder, examine well this face: yours, Sir, I well remember. Gaze on, and read in me your sister, Isabella.

MR. SEAL.   My sister!

ISAB.   But here's a claim more tender yet—your Indiana, Sir, your long-lost daughter.

MR. SEAL.   O my child! my child!

IND.   All-gracious heaven! is it possible! do I embrace my father!

MR. SEAL.   And do I hold thee? These passions are too strong for utterance. Rise, rise, my child, and give my tears their way.—O my Sister!   (*embracing her*)

ISAB.   Now, dearest Niece, my groundless fears, my painful cares no more shall vex thee. If I have wronged thy noble lover with too hard suspicions, my just concern for thee, I hope, will plead my pardon.

MR. SEAL.   Oh! make him, then, the full amends, and be yourself the messenger of joy. Fly this instant! tell him all these wondrous turns of Providence in his favour! Tell him I have now a daughter to bestow which he no longer will decline; that this day he still shall be a bridegroom; nor shall a fortune, the merit which his father seeks, be wanting; tell him the reward of all his virtues waits on his acceptance.

(*Exit* ISABELLA)

My dearest Indiana! (*turns and embraces her*)

IND.   Have I then, at last, a father's sanction on my love? his bounteous hand to give, and make my heart a present worthy of Bevil's generosity?

MR. SEAL.   O my child! how are our sorrows past o'erpaid by such a meeting! Though I have lost so many years of soft paternal dalliance with thee, yet, in one day to find thee thus, and thus bestow thee in such perfect happiness, is ample, ample reparation! And yet again, the merit of thy lover——

IND.   Oh, had I spirits left to tell you of his actions! how strongly filial duty has suppressed his love, and how concealment still has doubled all his obligations; the pride, the joy of his alliance, Sir, would warm your heart, as he has conquered mine.

MR. SEAL.   How laudable is love when born of virtue! I burn to embrace him——

IND.   See, Sir, my aunt already has succeeded, and brought him to your wishes.

Enter ISABELLA, *with* SIR JOHN BEVIL, BEVIL JUNIOR, MRS.

SIR J. BEV. (*entering*)   Where, where's this scene of wonder? Mr. Sealand, I congratulate, on this occasion, our mutual happiness. Your good sister, Sir, has, with the story of your daughter's fortune, filled us with surprise and joy. Now all exceptions are removed; my son has now avowed his love, and turned all former jealousies and doubts to approbation; and, I am told, your goodness has consented to reward him.

MR. SEAL.   If, Sir, a fortune equal to his father's hopes can make this object worthy his acceptance.

BEV. JUN.   I hear your mention, Sir, of fortune, with pleasure only as it may prove the means to reconcile the best of fathers to my love. Let him be provident, but let me be happy. — (*embracing* INDIANA) My ever-destined, my acknowledged wife!

IND.   Wife! Oh, my ever loved! my lord! my master!

SIR J. BEV.   I congratulate myself, as well as you, that I had a son who could, under such disadvantages, discover your great merit.

MR. SEAL.   O Sir John! how vain, how weak is human prudence! What care, what foresight, what imagination could contrive such blest events to make our children happy as Providence in one short hour has laid before us?

CIMB. (*to* MRS. SEALAND)   I am afraid, Madam, Mr. Sealand is a little too busy for our affair: if you please, we'll take another opportunity.

MRS. SEAL.   Let us have patience, Sir.

CIMB.   But we make Sir Geoffry wait, Madam.

MYRT.   O Sir! I am not in haste.

(*During this* BEVIL JUNIOR *presents* LUCINDA *to* INDIANA.)

MR. SEAL.   But here—here's our general benefactor! Excellent young man, that could be at once a lover to her beauty and a parent to her virtue.

BEV. JUN.   If you think that an obligation, Sir, give me leave to overpay myself, in the only instance that can now add to my felicity, by begging you to bestow this lady on Mr. Myrtle.

MR. SEAL.   She is his without reserve; I beg he may be sent for.—— Mr. Cimberton, notwithstanding you never had my consent, yet there is, since I last saw you, another objection to your marriage with my daughter.

CIMB.   I hope, Sir, your lady has concealed nothing from me?

MR. SEAL.   Troth, Sir! nothing but what was concealed from myself—another daughter, who has an undoubted title to half my estate.

CIMB.   How, Mr. Sealand! Why then, if half Mrs. Lucinda's fortune is gone, you can't say that any of my estate is settled upon her. I was in treaty for the whole, but if that is not to be come at, to be sure there can be no bargain. Sir,

I have nothing to do but to take my leave of your good lady, my cousin, and beg pardon for the trouble I have given this old gentleman.

MYRT. That you have, Mr. Cimberton, with all my heart.

(*discovers himself*)

OMN. Mr. Myrtle!

MYRT. And I beg pardon of the whole company that I assumed the person of Sir Geoffry, only to be present at the danger of this lady's being disposed of, and in her utmost exigence to assert my right to her; which, if her parents will ratify, as they once favoured my pretensions, no abatement of fortune shall lessen her value to me.

LUC. Generous man!

MR. SEAL. If, Sir, you can overlook the injury of being in treaty with one who as meanly left her as you have generously asserted your right in her, she is yours.

LUC. Mr. Myrtle, though you have ever had my heart, yet now I find I love you more because I bring you less.

MYRT. We have much more than we want, and I am glad any event has contributed to the discovery of our real inclinations to each other.

MRS. SEAL. (*aside*) Well! However, I'm glad the girl's disposed of, anyway.

BEV. JUN. Myrtle, no longer rivals now, but brothers!

MYRT. Dear Bevil, you are born to triumph over me. But now our competition ceases; I rejoice in the pre-eminence of your virtue, and your alliance adds charms to Lucinda.

SIR J. BEV. Now, ladies and gentlemen, you have set the world a fair example. Your happiness is owing to your constancy and merit, and the several difficulties you have struggled with evidently show

Whate'er the generous mind itself denies,

The secret care of Providence supplies.   (*Exeunt*)

EPILOGUE

By MR. WELSTED

INTENDED TO BE SPOKEN BY INDIANA

Our author, whom intreaties cannot move,
Spite of the dear coquetry that you love,
Swears he'll not frustrate (so he plainly means),
By a loose'epilogue, his decent scenes.
Is it not, Sirs, hard fate I meet to-day,
To keep me rigid still beyond the play?
And yet I'm sav'd a world of pains that way.
I now can look, I now can move at ease,
Nor need I torture these poor limbs to please,
Nor with the hand or foot attempt surprise,
Nor wrest my features, nor fatigue my eyes.
Bless me! what freakish gambols have I play'd!
What motions tried, and wanton looks betray'd!
Out of pure kindness all, to overrule
The threaten'd hiss, and screen some scribbling fool.
With more respect I'm entertain'd to-night:
Our author thinks I can with ease delight.
My artless looks while modest graces arm,
He says I need but to appear and charm.
A wife so form'd, by these examples bred,
Pours joy and gladness round the marriage bed;
Soft source of comfort, kind relief from care,
And 'tis her least perfection to be fair.
The nymph with Indiana's worth who vies,
A nation will behold with Bevil's eyes.